CONTEMPORARY

ASSESSMENT

AND TREATMENT OF ADULT CRIMINAL JUSTICE CLIENTS

CONTEMPORARY ASSESSMENT

AND TREATMENT OF ADULT CRIMINAL JUSTICE CLIENTS

FRANCIS J. DEISLER PH.D

TATE PUBLISHING & *Enterprises*

Published by Tate Publishing & Enterprises, LLC
127 E. Trade Center Terrace | Mustang, Oklahoma 73064 USA
1.888.361.9473 | www.tatepublishing.com

Tate Publishing is committed to excellence in the publishing industry. The company reflects the philosophy established by the founders, based on Psalm 68:11,
"The Lord gave the word and great was the company of those who published it."

Published in the United States of America

ISBN: 978-1-60696-391-3
Social Science / Criminology
09.03.16

DEDICATION

This book is dedicated to all professionals who have dedicated their careers to helping the criminal justice client get off the criminal justice merry-go-round.

ACKNOWLEDGMENTS

I owe thanks to all the criminal justice and mental health professionals that have contributed to my learning about treating criminal justice clients. I owe special thanks to my wife, two sons, and professional associates for their tolerance and understanding of my fixation and anxieties during the writing of this book. I owe thanks to the National Association of Forensic Counselors for allowing me the time off I needed to work on my manuscript. My wife, Karla, offered support and encouragement as well as reading and editing the final manuscript. Thank you.

I would like to thank Dr. Bret White and Dr. Mark Carich for working with me in a number of week long training workshops on sex offender assessment and treatment techniques as well as for how much I have learned from them. Thanks.

TABLE OF CONTENTS

PREFACE

In doing my trainings on treating criminal justice clients in state and federal prisons, probation, and parole departments, as well as for private practitioners in the field I am asked to recommend a textbook that applies to the criminal justice client specifically. As a result, I have reviewed many textbooks all of which directed themselves to specific subjects such as assessment, counseling theory, etc, but none provided a full picture of the criminal justice client and their special needs. Some provided a narrow orientation to understanding the criminal justice client based upon various theories of the causation of crime. I have never found a book designed for the mental health professional that included all the information that I as a practitioner with over thirty years experience specializing in the treatment of offenders that is unbiased and necessary in order to treat the criminal justice client competently. So, I decided to write about what I teach my trainees in the field of forensic counseling. In Chapter 1, I provide an overview of the various personality disorders that the overwhelming majority of criminal justice clients will present with which requires a well-trained and experienced therapist to deal with them effectively. I specialize in the assessment and treatment of personality disorders and have done all my clinical work in forensic residential, outpatient, and community-based private forensic facilities, and have used my experience to select the topics within this book.

As I wrote this book, I have kept in mind the complaints of my trainees who are not highly trained, or skilled about the lack of a comprehensive text that explains not so much of "what" to do, but rather, "what" and "how" to do it. The purpose of this book is to provide mental health professionals, criminal justice professionals, trainees, and students with the information and knowledge necessary to assess and "correct" the criminal justice client's thinking, feeling, and behaving. There is a lot of skepticism surrounding whether or not the criminal justice client can live a pro-social lifestyle, which I do not share. If we believe that nothing works, we will operate consistently with this belief, and prove it to be correct every time. However, if we believe that people can change, then we will treat our clients accordingly with that belief in mind, and we will also find that to be correct. Of course, you will, the same as I have, encounter some criminal justice clients that truly "nothing works."

The subject of this book encompasses a tremendous amount of information, which is necessary for the forensic therapist to know, as opposed to that which may be nice to know about criminal justice client assessment and treatment. I also hope that this book encourages mental health professionals and students that may be contemplating a career in forensic counseling to read much further on all the topics within this book and to involve themselves in a supervised forensic counseling training program.

Understanding

the Criminal Justice Client

For most therapists, the criminal justice client presents a diagnostic nightmare. This is because most therapists are not particularly skilled or trained in diagnosing and treating court mandated clients. They are generally professionals who the courts have referred clients to, and they are expected to do a job. Unlike a patient with a physical disorder, there are no laboratory tests to assist in diagnosing the criminal justice client for his or her behaviors. An accurate diagnosis only comes after a thorough psychological assessment and inquiry about their symptoms and mental well being. This is accomplished by the client providing an accurate medical, psychiatric, and social history, which may result in the client being referred for further evaluation. Diagnosis is difficult, as most court-referred clients appear to be indifferent about their life situation and control clinical interviews through deception and sometimes intimidation.

Offender Typologies
My clinical observation and experience is that there are basically three types of offenders that are generally referred by the courts or probation as follows: (a) a

first time offender that presents with no previous adult arrests, or juvenile status offenses. In many of these cases if there are no co-morbid psychiatric disorders, the arrest itself is a learning experience and the client never re-offends. However, if there is the presence of a conduct disorder, personality disorder, substance abuse disorder, or other psychiatric disorder, there is a strong probability that the first time offender will re-offend if intervention is not successful. (b) The second type of offender I refer to as the reactive recidivist. The reactive recidivist may have been arrested quite a few times as an adolescent and adult. However, a thorough assessment of this client will generally reveal that their criminal acting out behavior was in reaction to some psychosocial stressor such as a family problem, a death, loss of employment, financial problems, a separation or divorce which occurred up to six months prior to their being arrested. They generally offend later in life, and their offenses are generally impulsive acts. Their records will also reveal that they live law abiding and pro-social life styles between arrests. The reactive recidivist may, or may not have a co-occurring disorder. The most common co-occurring disorders found in this group of offenders that are linked to their criminal acting out are major affective disorders, anxiety disorders, alcohol abuse, or a dependent personality disorder. Rarely, if ever, is there sufficient evidence to assign a diagnosis of antisocial personality disorder. My clinical impression has always been that their offenses are a maladaptive resolution of life issues. (c) The final type of offender the court or probation department will refer for assessment and possible treatment is what I refer to as the multi-recidivist. The multi-recidivist will always present with a long history of childhood problems, social problems, adolescent status offenses such as runaways, petty thefts, minor in possession of illegal substances, numerous juvenile arrests, fighting, and violations of court ordered supervision. As an adult they are chronically unemployed, have poor social skills, have problems in their interpersonal relationships, may have been divorced two or more times, use and abuse alcohol and illegal substances, arrested numerous times, and may have served one or more jail or prison sentences, show evidence of deficits in their emotional expression, and utilize cognitive distortions. The multi-recidivist lacks affiliative orientation, as well as empathy, and is motivationally disorganized. They can be described as being psychologically ineffective. The multi-recidivist generally will meet the criteria for antisocial personality disorder and fit into one or more of the personality disorders discussed below. Approximately fifty percent of the multi- recidivists that are assessed will also have an alcohol or substance abuse diagnosis co-occurring with the antisocial personality disorder. Approximately ten to twelve percent will have a co-occurring psychiatric disorder.

Normal Offenders

Believe it or not there are criminal justice clients that do not suffer from a psychiatric or psychological disorder, and were well socialized as children with personalities within the normal range. Although most criminal justice clients insist they are innocent of the charge they were convicted of, some are in fact innocent, wrongly convicted and not criminals. Others may have been victims of an isolated confrontational situation resulting in bodily harm to another where they had no choice but to react for their own safety and were charged with a crime anyway. Many minorities who are faced with the choice of working for a minimum wage and living poorly, or making thousands of dollars dealing drugs and living well many times fall into this category. The point is that not all criminal justice clients walking in the front door of an agency is abnormal.

The Antisocial Personality Disorder

When a client is referred by the court system, it has practically become synonymous with the diagnosis of antisocial personality disorder (APD) because of their criminal acting out behavior. They are seen as people that are not insane, and they know the difference between right and wrong. According to some researchers, they may be choosing not to control their urges to act out, Samenow, 1998. Although Dr. Samenow stresses the importance of understanding the criminal's thinking, as well as how they choose to act out, in his book *Inside the Criminal Mind* there is no explanation as to why criminals make the wrong choices they do.

APD is the most common diagnosis for the criminal population, which may or may not be productive. According to the American Psychiatric Associations (APA) Diagnostic Statistical Manual - IV (DSM), "the essential features of APD include consistent patterns of behaviors that have total disregard for, as well as the violation of the rights of others occurring since age fifteen, as indicated by three or more of the following: (a) failure to conform to social norms with respect to law-

16

ful behaviors as indicated by repeatedly performing acts that are grounds for arrest, (b) deceitfulness, as indicated by repeated lying, uses of aliases, or conning others for personal profit or pleasure, (c) impulsiveness or failure to plan ahead, (d) irritability and aggressiveness, as indicated by repeated physical fights, or assaults, (e) reckless disregard for safety of self or others, (f) consistent irresponsibility as indicated by repeated failure to sustain consistent work behavior or honor financial obligations, and (g) lack of remorse, as indicated by being indifferent to or rationalizing having hurt, mistreated, or stolen from another. "To allocate the diagnosis of APD, the individual must be at least eighteen years of age. However, the symptoms of APD often begin in childhood and early adolescence continuing well into adulthood. Many children show aggression toward their peers, as well as animals. They violate rules, steal, and are deceitful. They have a complete disregard for the rights of others. These children when identified are assigned the DSM-IV diagnosis of conduct disorder (CD). As these children grow into adulthood, they may pursue illegal activities and at the same time present to others as being very charming and appealing, but in reality they are very closed and opinionated, operating from an extremely rigid internal frame of reference, which restricts how they think, feel and behave in every life situation. Their rigid frames of reference make APD the most reliably diagnosed disorder amongst the personality disorders. However, the diagnosis of APD has been and continues to be controversial, primarily because the criteria has changed so many times with each new edition of the DSM (DSM-I 1968; DSM-II 1976; DSM-III

1980; DSM-III-R 1987; and finally DSM-IV 1994). The diagnosis of APD was to a large extent changed with the DSM-III 1980 edition when the APA distinguished the difference between child and adult characteristics and replaced a behavioral criteria for personality criteria. The next edition DSM-III-R 1987 the criteria again changed with the focus being on violence and a list of violent behaviors. The current DSM-IV criteria for APD basically says that anything that is not sociopathy, psychopathy or a dyssocial personality disorder is an antisocial personality disorder. In western society, APD occurs in approximately 3% of males and 1% of females according to the DSM-IV.

According to the literature, the occurrence of APD is twice as high in large inner cities thoughout the United States than in small towns, suburbs, or rural areas. It affects all social classes, but is more prominent amongst poor people. Persons born into wealthy families have the resources to channel their APD into a successful business or political career. Those less fortunate that are born into poor families tend to seek out criminal activities and end up in the criminal justice system on probation, or in the state correctional system. Since African-Americans are 70% more likely to be incarcerated within the correctional system, it would be reasonable to assume that the incidence of APD must be high among African-Americans. However, there are definitely other reasons for the high incidence crime among African-Americans such as poverty, lack of educational opportunities, unemployment, discrimination, lack of basic needs and racism. Whether White, Black, Hispanic, Asian, or other ethnicity, it doesn't matter. If a crime was committed and the person was incarcerated they share the APD diagnosis. It doesn't take very much to make that diagnostic impression stick; all it takes is a juvenile record, an adult offense, evidence of aggressiveness, impulsivity, or poor work history.

The diagnosis of APD many times results in the missing of co-morbid psychiatric disorders that co-occur with the APD such as alcohol abuse and substance abuse whose diagnostic behaviors are very similar. It also masks other serious psychiatric disorders such as bi-polar disorder, anxiety disorder, schizophrenia or other undiagnosed Axis I and II disorders. There hasn't been very much research on APD and the co morbidity of other psychiatric disorders. Most of the research, and there is very little of that, has been on APD and substance abuse. From those studies, it appears that in the majority of persons that are addicted to substances, APD preceded the substance addiction, and in some case, the addiction had led to APD behaviors. Other disorders associated with APD may also include gambling addiction, as well as features of narcissistic personality disorder.

So what are the causes of antisocial personality disorder? There have been numerous studies, but the causes of APD are still unknown. There have been studies trying to draw a physiological link between behaviors during pregnancy or other chemical or viral agent affecting the embryo or fetus during development, or a hereditary link. However these studies had no significant P-values, and none have been proven. My clinical impression based upon my thirty years of specializing in the assessment and treatment of this population is that the development of APD is primarily the result of either poor parenting practices or exposure to a poor environment, or a combination of both.

Historically, researchers as well as clinicians have used numerous terms including moral insanity, psychopathy, and sociopathy to describe the APD, even though each are distinctly different pathologies requiring different treatment approaches. The symptoms of these disorders which are considered the key elements of the APD have historically evolved from the focal point of a lack of emotional attachment in relationships, Cleckley 1964, to a focus on the individual's observable behaviors, especially aggressive and impulsive behaviors (APA 1994).The current DSM-IV description of the APD is not a very useful term because it describes the individual solely on the basis of their disobedience to society. The diagnosis of APD today is practically synonymous with criminal behavior when in reality it is probable that the largest majority of the APD population are law-abiding people who do not agree with many social rules or values, which in today's world would assign an extremely large portion of society as having APD. Many criminologists and mental health clinicians often refer to APD as a garbage can diagnosis, which is used when no other explanation for the client's behavior is found.

The differences between APD, sociopathy and psychopathy are clearly defined by the severity of their behaviors that are progressive and become chronic, resulting in dysfunction in major life areas. As I stated above, the APD for the most part is a rule breaker that doesn't agree with many social rules and values, and may violate the law or commit a low-level crime. However, the person suffering with sociopathy is a different story altogether, because the disorder is chiefly characterized by a lack of conscience. They seem to be able to neutralize any sense of conscience or time perspective by focusing on the present and ignoring past experiences with no regard for the future. They only care about fulfilling their own wants and needs, and are egocentric to an extreme. Others are seen as objects to be used in getting their wants and needs fulfilled. Their thinking is "what you have is mine for the taking." If by chance they should give something back, in return it is only a scheme to take even more.

The Borderline Personality

Another common personality disturbance observed in the criminal justice client is the Borderline Personality, which is estimated to afflict about 2% of the general population, about 10% among individuals seen in outpatient mental health settings, and about 20% among psychiatric inpatients. It is estimated that 3–5% of persons referred by the criminal justice system presenting with a substance abuse disorder are Borderline Personality Disorders (BPD). Both the APD and BPD client are extremely manipulative. The primary difference between APD and BPD is those with APD manipulate others to gain profit, power, control, or some other gratification, while the BPD's goal is directed more toward gaining the concern of caretakers and others.

The Borderline Personality Disorder is defined in the DSM-IV as a pervasive pattern of instability in interpersonal relationships, self-image, and affects, and marked impulsivity beginning by early adulthood and present in a variety of contexts, as indicated by five or more of the following: (a) frantic efforts to avoid real or imagined abandonment, (b) a pattern of unstable and intense interpersonal relationships characterized by alternating between extremes of idealization and devaluation, (c) identity disturbance: markedly and persistently unstable self-image or sense of self, (d) impulsiveness in at least two areas that are potentially self-damaging (e.g. spending, sex, substance abuse, reckless driving, binge eating), (e) recurrent suicidal behavior, gestures, or threats, or self-mutilating behavior, (f) affect instability due to a marked reactivity of mood (e.g. intense episodic dysphoria, irritability, or anxiety usually lasting a few hours and only rarely more than a few days), (g) chronic feelings of emptiness, (h) inappropriate, intense anger or difficulty controlling anger (e.g. frequent displays of anger, constant anger, recurrent physical fights), and (i) transient, stress related paranoid ideation or severe dissociative symptoms.

Individuals with BPD will generally present with a history of emotional, physical, and/or sexual abuse, substance abuse disorders, or a major affective disorder. They are extremely difficult to treat because the therapist-client relationship is subject to the same inappropriate and unrealistic demands that they place on all interpersonal relationships.

The Narcissistic Personality Disorder

Narcissistic Personality Disorder (NPD) is most often diagnosed with another disorder, especially impulse control disorders or a substance abuse disorder. The NPD and the APD both lack empathy and disregard social rules. However, the APD carries their disregard for society to the extreme and is more likely to be more manipulative, calculating, and unfeeling. Their abusive and criminal acting out behaviors are generally not intended and thought-out like the APD, sociopath, or psychopaths. In the majority of cases diagnosed as APD there are NPD features more often than not making treatment more difficult. The prognosis for an adult suffering from NPD is poor, although their adaptation to life and others may improve with treatment.

The DSM-IV defines NPD as a pervasive pattern of grandiosity (in fantasy or behavior), need for admiration, and lack of empathy beginning by early adulthood and present in a variety of contexts as indicated by five or more of the following items:(a) has a grandiose sense of self-importance (e.g. exaggerates achievements and talents, expects to be recognized as superior without commemorate achievements), (b) is preoccupied with fantasies of unlimited success, power, brilliance, beauty, or ideal love, (c) believes that he or she is special and unique and can only be understood by, or should associate with, other special or high-status people (or institutions), (d) requires excessive admiration, (e) has a sense of entitlement, i.e. unreasonable expectations of especially favorable treatment or automatic compliance with his or her expectations, (f) is interpersonally exploitative, i.e. takes advantage of others to achieve his or her own ends, (g) lacks empathy: is unwilling to recognize or identify with the feelings and needs of others, (h) is often envious of others or believes that others are envious of him or her, and (i) shows arrogant, haughty behaviors or attitudes.

The Sociopathic Personality

Cleckley (1964) probably provides the most accurate description of the sociopathic personality based on his extensive experience. Cleckley describes the sociopath as being superficially charming, of good intelligence; absence of delusions and irrational thinking; the absence of "nervousness" or neurotic manifestations; unreliable; untruthful and insincere; lack of remorse; antisocial behavior without compunction; poor judgment and does not learn from experiences; pathologic egocentricity and incapacity for love; general poverty in major affective reactions; specific loss of insight; unresponsiveness in general interpersonal relations; fantastic and uninviting behavior with drink, and sometimes without; suicide threats rarely carried out; sex life impersonal, trivial, and poorly integrated; failure to follow any life plan.

Many sociologists and psychologists today believe that the unsocialized personality of the sociopath is due to parental failures rather than an innate feature of their character. The more severe the sociopathic behavior is, the more likely it is that there was parental deprivation (Craft, Stephenson, and Granger, 1964). When parental deprivation is present, it is not unusual that many developmental wants and needs were not met also, such as:

- The basic need for shelter, food, and clothing
- Love and nurturing
- Emotional support
- Security and protection
- Established boundaries and structure
- Discipline and consistency

- Safe environment
- Exploration and play
- Support in being creative

According to (Lykken, 1995) there are at least four different subtypes of sociopaths: the common, alienated, aggressive, and dyssocial types. The common type is characterized by their lack of conscience and are generally career type criminals which appear to be increasing in our society primarily because of incompetent parenting; the alienated type by their inability to love and to accept love; the aggressive type which is characterized mostly by their consistent sadistic tendencies; and the dyssocial type marked by their ability in seeking out and adapting to a subculture such as a street gang whose rules are clearly antisocial. It is important to be aware that regardless of what type of sociopath a criminal may be, they all rationalize or justify their behaviors. A list of sociopathic traits that may assist in identifying the sociopathic personality, of which according to (Stout, 1996) only three are needed are as follows:

- Egocentricity
- Impulsivity
- Callousness
- Defect of conscience
- Risk taking
- Excessive boasting
- Exaggerated sexuality
- Inability to resist temptation
- Deprecating attitude toward the opposite sex

The Concept of Psychopathy

The concept of psychopathy has been the subject of debate for decades, and is usually defined as a group of affective, interpersonal, and behavioral characteristics including; lack of impulse control; irresponsibility; shallow emotions; lack of empathy; lack of guilt or remorse; pathological lying; conning; and the persistent violation of social norms and expectations (Hare 1993; Cleckley 1964). The term psychopath actually means, "psychologically damaged." Crimes committed by psychopaths are different from crimes committed by the APD or sociopath. They are predators that generally commit violent crimes causing physical harm or death without any feelings of remorse, or for any apparent reason. They take what they want and do what they want without guilt or remorse, satisfying their hunger for power and control. For example, a sociopath committing an armed robbery would take what they wanted and leave the scene of the crime, but the psychopath would take what they wanted and then kill everyone so as not to leave any witnesses before they left. That act of violence is what differentiates the sociopath from the psychopath. They are considered untreatable predators whose violence is well planned, and emotionless. Their emotionless replicates an isolated, fearless and anxiety free dissociated state that according to some researchers may reveal a lower autonomic nervous system. They cannot be understood in terms of early life developmental interferences as can the APD; they are truly morally depraved predators that represent the worst in any civilized society. All psychopaths are antisocial personalities, but not all antisocial personalities are psychopaths.

While most civilized societies regard psychopaths as criminals, there are societies where they are looked upon as being heroes, patriots, martyrs, and even great leaders. An example of this is the recruitment of terrorists who are willing to kill themselves and others without empathy or hesitation. They are morally deprived psychopaths because their acts of violence victimize innocent people. Most people don't kill, and can contain their urges to harm others; however, those that cannot contain themselves and lack empathy for others such as suicide bombers are psychopathic.

The concept of psychopathy is extremely complex, because not all psychopaths are categorized the same. Cleckley made the first distinction between psychopath typologies. He described the differences between a primary and secondary psychopath. Let's take a look at the differences between Cleckley's primary and secondary psychopath.

The Primary Psychopath

The primary psychopath according to Cleckley does not respond to punishment or disapproval, and experience little or no apprehension or stress. They are capable of presenting themselves in a very positive manner, inhibiting their antisocial impulses to achieve their purpose. The primary psychopath does not respond to words the same as others, as they do not seem to have the same meaning for the psychopath as they do for us. It seems as though they do not understand the meaning of their own words, a condition described by Cleckley as "semantic aphasia." They experience no genuine emotions, have no goals, and do not follow any life plan. According to

Lykken (1995), they may resemble the unsocialized products of incompetent parenting and bad environments but, because they are so resistant to socialization, they derive also from middle class, traditional families with long suffering parents who have attempted to provide good opportunities.

The Secondary Psychopath

The secondary psychopath was identified in the middle 1980s and is described as being a risk taker. However, they are also more likely to experience guilt, stress, and excessive worries. Because they are risk takers, they will expose themselves to more stressful situations than do others. As their anxiety increases toward an unlawful act or object, so does their attraction to it increase. They do not like pain and are driven to avoid it. They are unable to resist temptation, and live their lives by the lure of temptation. They are an extremely unconventional, daring, and adventurous group who started playing by their own rules in life at a very age. Since Cleckley's work on psychopath typologies, other researchers, as well as criminologists have identified several other subtypes, which include the distempered psychopath and the charismatic psychopath as follows:

The Distempered Psychopath

The distempered psychopath is described as an individual that can easily become enraged more quickly than the other psychopath subtypes. They have extremely strong sex drives, are capable of extremely high sexual energy, and obsessed by sexual urges during most of the day. Their urges and cravings led them into alcohol

abuse, substance abuse, gambling, kleptomania, pedophilia, and other illegal activities. They enjoy the adren-
alin rush they get from their risk taking. Serial killers,
serial rapists, and serial pedophiles can be described as
distempered psychopaths.

The Charismatic Psychopath

The charismatic psychopath can be described as being
charming, attractive, irresistible, and pathological liars.
They are conning and seem to possess the ability to
swindle others out of everything they own, sometimes
even their lives as have been seen in some religious cults.
The charismatic psychopath seems to believe in himself
and his fictions, which makes their victims even more
vulnerable to be victimized.

One other group of psychopaths that (Lykken, 1995)
refers to based upon his clinical work is the Hysterical
Psychopath. According to Lykken, this particular type
of psychopath sometimes show signs of the psychopath's
impassiveness to the consequences of their deeds, but at
times, displays normal feelings of anxiety, guilt, and even
remorse for their earlier behavior. All of the psychopath
subtypes discussed share some common traits, such as
being predators, persistence, emotionless, controlling,
and a capacity for violence. In one way or another, each
type tends to operate with a grandiose demeanor, an
extremely high level of entitlement, a rapacious tendency
toward sadism, as well as a severely contaminated frame
of reference which is utilized to define themselves, others, and society in general. According to (Lykken, 1995)
the core characteristic of all the psychopath subtypes

seems to be fearlessness, as well as a severe lack of psychological effectiveness (Deisler, 2002).

Psychological Effectiveness

According to (McCall, 1975), psychological effectiveness has at least two specific requirements designated as "cognitive adequacy" and "motivational organization." Cognitive adequacy has two components referred to as "self-understanding" and "reality contact." Motivational organization also possesses two requirements referred to as "self direction" and "emotional integration." Self-Understanding is what we generally refer to as self-awareness, which is how we perceive our world and ourselves. This awareness of one's own being and function leads to a sense of self, which is labeled self-concept. Self-understanding is extremely important because it is an organized, dynamic, and theoretical pattern of an individual's perception of themselves in relation to others experienced in their environment, and the values attached to those perceptions. In short, reality contact is simply one's perception of their world, which is an accurate observation of their external world at the time, and their experiences in the world. Unfortunately, the sociopaths and psychopaths early life experiences were mostly negative which they generalized to include the whole world and everyone in it. Their perception of self is primarily based upon early negative life experiences and teaching which they continue to utilize in the present. Self-understanding, self-awareness, and self-concept are not enough to assure psychological effectiveness; however, it is impossible without it.

The next area of concern in the lack of psychological

effectiveness is self-direction, which is severely impaired for the APD, sociopath, and psychopath alike. All of us must direct our thinking, feeling, and actions ourselves, or accept the direction of others. Self-direction is necessary in order for one to direct themselves and to achieve their full potential. Without the aptitude to direct themselves severely impairs their ability to establish any short or long-term goals in their life. Primarily because of poor parenting practices the APD, sociopath, and psychopath appear impaired in their ability to direct their thinking and behaviors in socially acceptable ways, and as a result require direction from others, which they rarely accept. As a young child, dependence upon others does not allow many choices, because good parenting requires that we direct the child in making the right choices, and developing socially acceptable rules, values, beliefs, and rewarding the resulting pro-social behaviors.

The APD, Sociopath, and Psychopath's lack of emotional integration results in what (McCall, 1975) refers to as a lack of affiliative orientation, which excludes any type of dependence upon others. Without affiliative orientation, there is no interdependence upon others, which is required in our society, and results in a lack of empathy, which permits them to commit their crimes without any feelings of guilt, shame, or remorse. Without affiliative orientation, empathy is not possible, and therefore, their victims are perceived as not being like them, and as a result, whatever they have is theirs for the taking without any concern for the safety or welfare for the victim. Their lack of affiliative orientation excludes their ability to identify with their victim, or to experience sensations, thoughts, feelings, and emotions as experienced by others. Affiliative orientation and empathy are learned behaviors that most of us have been fortunate enough to achieve as a result of good parenting practices. Therefore, a major issue in treating offenders is the development of psychological effectiveness. The lack of psychological effectiveness results in major deficits in the following areas:

- A lack of self-understanding or insight
- A lack of being cognizant of others in their individual and institutional roles
- Unaware of the future and unfeeling to the present
- A lack of emotional stability
- A lack of emotional commitment or responsiveness to others
- A lack of commitment to short-term or long-term goals

My clinical experience with clients presenting the above deficits in psychological effectiveness also demonstrates a lack of both social and impulse control in almost all life areas, (Deisler, 2002). At this point, the reader should clearly be able to recognize the above issues as being common among the majority of court-referred clients seen in counseling that are diagnosed as CD, APD, sociopathic or psychopathic. All of the above deficits in psychological effectiveness should be addressed on the client's treatment plan. Failure to do so will most likely result in the offender re-offending.

Progression from APD to Psychopathy

In my own clinical work, I have encountered many psychopathic subtypes and believe that there is a progression from childhood to full-blown psychopathy in many individuals who at one time displayed normal feelings and empathy toward others. My clinical impression has been that psychopathy originally presents itself in its early stages during childhood, going unnoticed, and not presenting for clinical attention until adolescence when they may be labeled a conduct disorder as a result of coming into contact with the juvenile criminal justice system, or even adulthood as their behavior becomes even more severe. The progression is from conduct disorder, to antisocial personality disorder sociopathy, and finally psychopathy. Each stage is observable in the frequency, intensity, and severity of their behaviors.

Case Example of Progression from CD to Psychopathy

Jason is a thirty-three-year-old Caucasian male originally seen in counseling by me in 1984 at age nine. He was referred by his school counselor because of his poor adjustment, skipping classes, and aggressive behavior toward his schoolmates. Jason is one of forty-two clients that I have been tracking as part of my study on progression. Jason's parents were divorced prior to his age four, his mother having full custody of Jason. Jason's father has not been involved with Jason since the divorce and does not contribute to his support. His mother refused to participate in the counseling process with Jason, or to cooperate with school authorities. No evidence of alcoholism, drug abuse, physical or sexual abuse was evident at first because of the lack of parental cooperation and Jason's refusal to talk about his family. However, based upon information that we were able to collect from the school and other official records from child protective services, as well as the family court, we were able to establish that Jason's father was alcoholic and there was evidence of both physical and emotional abuse from both parents toward Jason.

Jason was evaluated by me and participated in several interviews with our psychiatrist. Jason was found to be of average intelligence, no evidence of any learning disabilities or other gross psychopathologies that would interfere with his social functioning. Because of his consistent pattern of acting out behaviors, which involved fighting, petty theft, lying, and truancy, a diagnosis of conduct disorder was applied.

Jason was seen on a weekly basis individually and eventually in group therapy with children in the same school grade and age range as him for thirteen months by our clinical social worker who specializes in childhood conduct disorders. Jason progressed well during his thirteen -month treatment sharing his feelings of abandonment by his father, as well as his hurt because of his mother's lack of affection and support toward him. Jason articulated appropriate feelings, made positive changes in his behaviors toward others, developed coping strategies to effectively deal with his home situation, and did extremely well in his schoolwork passing all his classes with above average grades. Jason was eventually terminated from treatment at age eleven.

The next time Jason was seen at our agency was at his age eighteen when he was referred by the court for armed robbery, battery, possession of a fire arm, possession of a controlled substance, and violation of probation for a previous offense of burglary committed at his age fourteen for which he was placed on five years probation which he violated on two separate occasions at his age of sixteen and seventeen for minor in possession of alcohol. Again, Jason was evaluated and was diagnosed as a primary Axis II antisocial personality disorder because his consistent patterns of behavior were present long before his use of any alcohol or drugs. A secondary Axis I diagnosis of alcohol abuse and cocaine abuse was assigned because evaluation results indicated that he began abusing alcohol and substances at his age 16, long after he first presented with behavioral problems. It was determined that the use of alcohol and other substances was the result of Jason's present lifestyle. Jason was eventually adjudicated, found guilty of all offenses, and sentenced to ten years in a state correctional facility.

Jason served approximately half his prison sentence before making parole and returning to his mother's home. Jason failed to fulfill his parole obligations by assaulting a police officer that stopped him for questioning about a rape and armed robbery, which happened in the area. Again, Jason was arrested and convicted and sentenced to a fifteen-year prison term in a maximum-security facility. This time Jason served almost twelve years on his fifteen-year sentence because of his assaultive behavior toward other inmates and prison staff. Jason was released after serving eleven years and eleven months, at which time he returned to his community where he has resided all his life. Jason didn't last long after his release from prison; he was arrested for armed robbery, rape, and double homicide within six months after release. Jason robbed a local convenience store raping a female clerk and female customer. After the robbery and rapes, Jason killed both victims so as to not leave any witnesses against him. He was identified because of several security cameras inside and outside the convenience store.

I was retained by Jason's defense attorney, a public defender who was filled to capacity with cases and was sympathetic toward Jason's early life problems. I was retained to do a death sentence mitigation evaluation in hopes of dropping the possibility of a death sentence to a life sentence because of my familiarity with Jason. There were certainly many mitigating circumstances in Jason's life, and he eventually was sentenced to fifty years to life rather than the death penalty.

Stories like Jason's are not uncommon. You can clearly see the progression from conduct disorder to APD, Sociopathy, and eventually full-blown psychopathy. The behaviors become more and more severe, and increase in frequency resulting in some form of tissue damage such as rape, assaults, and eventually homicide. For those individuals progressing to psychopathy, as did Jason, eventually a lengthy prison term or life imprisonment is not unusual.

Conduct Disorder

My clinical experience has been that conduct disorders can be successfully treated. Short of committing a homicide, there is nothing that a young person has done up to this point in their life that they cannot successfully recover from and go on to live a normal productive life. However, in order for recovery to be successful, early intervention and treatment must occur. Part of the problem in identifying CD in its early stages is who is identifying it. This presents a serious problem in early identification, because different social systems utilize different terms, and focus on different characteristics of a child's problem behaviors. The educational system uses the term "socially maladjusted" when referring to problematic children. The juvenile criminal justice system uses the term "juvenile delinquent" when referring to a problematic child. Regardless of the terms used, the identified behaviors most often are very closely associated with the mental health definition of conduct disorder. This happens because it is sometimes easier for the educational system or the legal system to explain away the problem behaviors, or to even normalize the behaviors that are in reality abnormal because of a child's young age without having a mental health evaluation, and thereby avoiding early intervention.

When the behaviors continue or become more severe, the educational system will continue to evaluate the child as having a social problem that requires discipline in the form of after school detention, suspension, or expulsion. The legal system on the other hand will determine that the child is behaving in a criminal way, and most times believes the appropriate intervention should be punishment by placing the child on probation, community service work, or even incarceration. The significance of the lack of effectiveness is obvious. Whoever initially encounters and evaluates the child, determines the diagnosis and course of treatment. Therefore, early intervention by mental health professionals is crucial in order for there to be a positive prognosis (Toth, 1990).

As I mentioned earlier, conduct disorder is the beginning of a long hard trip through APD, sociopathy and psychopathy if intervention fails. This means that caution must be employed during the evaluation process to assure an accurate diagnosis is made, and appropriate treatment strategies are utilized. For example, severe family pathology is frequent in most cases of CD and it is difficult to unravel if the adolescent's behavior contributed to the family's pathology, or if the family itself was pathological prior to having the child, which may make a crucial contribution to the primary diagnosis of CD and even a differential diagnosis.

According to the Diagnostic and Statistical Manual of Mental Disorders (DSM-IV) the essential feature of Conduct Disorder (CD) is a repetitive and persistent pattern of behavior in which the basic rights of others or major age-appropriate societal norms or rules are violated. According to the DSM-IV these behaviors fall into the following four subtypes; (1) aggressive conduct toward other people or animals, (2) non-aggressive conduct that causes property loss or damage, (3) deceitfulness or theft, and (4) serious violations of rules.

The CD becomes more obvious during adolescence as the behaviors become more severe, and generally comes to the attention of law enforcement at some level. It is not uncommon during these early years to observe the Conduct Disorders illegal behaviors increase in severity from serious violations of rules, to conning and theft, to aggressive conduct toward others including battery, robbery, rape, or even homicide. Those adolescents presenting with a persistent pattern of aggressive behaviors also seem to lack any feelings of guilt, shame, or remorse for their behaviors, and lack any empathy toward others. My clinical impression has always been that when a CD presents with this progressive pattern of aggressive behaviors, that this was a precursor to psychopathy. Unfortunately, these days we encounter more and more adolescents in treatment that appear to fit this criteria because of parenting practices resulting in poor socialization. According to many psychologists and sociologists socialization involves: (1) supervising a child's behavior, (2) being aware of the child's activities, (3) identifying antisocial behaviors when they do occur, (4) disciplining the child for the behavior, (5) modeling and encouraging pro-social behaviors, (6) rewarding pro-social behavior, (7) teaching the child what is right and what is wrong. When parents neglect these responsibilities, and there is no community resource to carry out the socializing role, then CD, APD, Sociopathy, or even Psychopathy can be the expected outcome.

Fortunately, not all adolescents that are conduct disordered become psychopaths. A lot of them become socialized through outside controls such as being in the military, the development of positive peer relations, involvement in sports and other pro-social activities. But unfortunately those children that are aggressive, tough, fearless, have violent tempers, are highly sexed, etc, will most likely progress to APD, Sociopathy, or Psychopathy and in due course to prison.

Diagnostic Considerations

Mental health professionals taking on the role of diagnostician must be qualified through education, training, experience, supervision, and skills in diagnosing criminal justice clients. Mental health professionals are discouraged from diagnosing that which does not meet those criteria. They must possess adequate knowledge which includes: (a) an understanding the nature of CD, APD, Sociopathy, Psychopathy, its pathology and progression, (b) the ability to distinguish accurately the common symptoms of CD, APD, Sociopathy and Psychopathy in a person who appears to be suffering from these pathologies from other disorders that may appear similar, (c) identification of the underlying developmental interferences that may have caused the pathology, (d) knowledge of the pathologies personal, social, family, legal, educational, vocational and spiritual consequences, (e) accurate interpretation of assessment data, and (f) the ability to briefly and accurately state in writing the diagnostic conclusion, the assessment data utilized, observations and other data on which it is based, and recommendations for referral and treatment.

The simplest theoretical framework to diagnose CD, APD, Sociopathy, or Psychopathy is a consistent pattern of legal violations and a violation of the rights of others. However, this approach to diagnosis has historically resulted in confusing APD symptoms with other pathologies that imitate the symptoms of APD such as alcohol or other drug abuse.

There is a great deal of unpredictability in the types of co-morbid psychiatric disorders among criminal justice clients that can confuse a primary APD diagnosis. Some common examples include schizophrenia, borderline personality disorder, panic disorder, major affective disorder, and alcohol or drug abuse. These disorders have the intrinsic power to alter considerably the way one thinks, feels, and behaves. According to Regier, et al, (1990) more than fifty percent of clients presenting with a substance abuse disorder have sufficient symptoms to be diagnosed with another psychiatric disorder. Therefore, a diagnostician must have a thorough understanding of both the pathology of APD and its presenting symptoms as well as other psychiatric disorders. The confusing presentation of similar psychiatric symptoms requires the skill of determining which came first, the symptoms, or the behavior. For example, when a court referred client presents with both the symptoms of APD and a drug abuse disorder, the clinician should do a timeline to determine which occurred first, the APD symptoms and related problems, or the use of drugs. If the client's behavioral symptoms were present prior to the use of drugs, the primary diagnosis would be APD, and the drug abuse diagnosis would be secondary to the APD.

Making the distinction between the primary and secondary diagnosis when present, is extremely important as it has an effect on the development of the treatment plan, prognosis, and treatment of the criminal justice client. Without a doubt, a positive prognosis and treatment outcome for a primary alcoholic or drug-abusing client is more encouraging than for a primary APD, Sociopath, or Psychopath. In summary, both primary and necessary diagnostic symptoms for the diagnosis of APD are those observable common and particular effects that are caused directly by the underlying APD psychopathology, and that as a result demonstrate the existence of antisocial personality disorder.

When the primary diagnosis of APD is formulated, it

also indicates limitations to the possibility of treatment approaches; it suggests that long-term intense psychotherapy would be most appropriate based on the length and severity of the pathology. It also indicates the need to carefully evaluate how to structure the offender's daily life while such intensive therapy proceeds. Based upon the length and severity of the offender's psychopathology, the possibility may have to be accepted that they may require one to three years of intense therapy.

Another factor to be considered in diagnosing APD is family and cultural features. According to the literature as well as the DSM-IV (1994) antisocial personality disorder appears to be associated with low socioeconomic status and urban settings. There are also concerns that the diagnosis of APD at times may be misapplied to individuals in settings in which seemingly antisocial behavior may be part of a protective survival strategy. It also appears that APD is more common among first-degree biological relatives of those with APD than among the general population. Therefore, in both the assessment and diagnosis of APD, it is useful for the clinician to also consider the family history as well as the social and economic environment in which the behaviors occur.

Family Pattern

Antisocial Personality Disorder, sociopathy, and psychopathy are more frequently found among first-degree biological relatives with the same disorder than among the general population. The biological relatives of persons with these disorders are also at risk for substance abuse related disorders compared with the general population. Studies indicating a possible genetic predisposition to alcoholism and other substances are often cited to support this position. One such study by (Parsian and Cloninger, 1991) found that adopted children with alcoholic biological parents were more likely to become alcoholic, than adopted children with biological parents that are nonalcoholic. According to the DSM-IV, 1994, biological relatives of persons with antisocial personality disorder are also at increased risk for Somatization Disorder; however, this is more common among females. Children live in their adult lives what they have learned. A family environment where a biological or adoptive parent has an antisocial personality disorder, influences and puts at high risk the likelihood of a child developing a personality disorder and its related psychopathology.

FORENSIC ASSESSMENT

OF ADULT OFFENDERS COURT MANDATED

ASSESSMENT AND TREATMENT

It is an uncommon occurrence for a client to seek treatment on their own that is addicted to alcohol, drugs, or committing a crime. They don't a have spontaneous insight into their lifestyles and other life problems and seek help. The vast majority of clients with CD, APD, Sociopathy, or Psychopathy are referred by the criminal justice system for assessment or treatment, or from parole release authorities as a condition of their parole release. When these clients are ordered to submit to an evaluation or treatment, will intervention and treatment be effective? According to (Royce, 1989) properly done interventions succeed ninety-seven percent of the time in getting the person into treatment. This has not been my clinical experience with the majority of court-referred clients. My experience has been that the client's age, type of offenses, criminal history, number of incarcerations, and severity of other life problems are all factors affecting success or failure in assessment, intervention and directing a client into treatment. However, I can say that in approximately half of the clients that have been assessed, intervention was successful.

According to (Matuschka, 1985), "treatment which carried a coercive element has been shown to have a higher cure ratio than treatment without a coercive element" (p. 209). A wide variety of other studies (Goldcamp and Weiland, 1993) as well as (Anglin, et al, 1989) have studied the effectiveness of court-mandated treatment for offenders, and came to the conclusion that court mandated clients do as well or even better than voluntary clients.

Initial Client Contact

Initial client contact occurs at the time of intake. Unfortunately, for most community based forensic outpatient programs, intake is generally having the client complete paperwork consisting of demographic face sheets, medical history forms, financial agreements, insurance information, and agency rules. For most treatment populations this process may be appropriate; however, for the criminal justice client it leaves many loopholes open for manipulation.

Many obstacles to treating the offender can be overcome at the time of intake. Criminal justice clients being treated in community based forensic programs are not voluntary. There is almost always a set of conditions that are mandated and enforced by the referring court, stipulating certain parameters of their treatment and other aspects of their life while within the court's jurisdiction, which assists in treatment compliance. In addition to the criminal justice client completing their initial paperwork, the client should be required to sign a treatment contract which clearly describes all therapeutic activities they may or may not be required to participate in, including but not limited to the following: (a) assessment, (b) evaluation, (c) psycho-educational classes, (d) individual, group, family therapy, (e) participation in support groups, (f) relapse prevention planning, and, (g) random urinalysis, or polygraph examination to monitor program and treatment compliance.

The treatment contract should also clearly define what will be expected from the client while they are in treatment including but not limited to: (a) full program participation, (b) taking responsibility for their present offense, (c) remaining alcohol and drug free, (d) following all treatment recommendations, and (e) payment of fees. The treatment contract should be clear about all requirements and expectations including the limitations on confidentiality. The treatment contract should be signed by the client, the intake worker, and assigned therapist. The client and their probation/parole agent should be provided with a copy of the contract, and a copy entered into the medical record. A sample treatment contract, which you may consider utilizing, is available in appendix A of this text.

There are certain legal requirements providing treatment to criminal justice clients, which are significant. One requirement includes confidentiality and duty to warn. On the issue of limited confidentiality the criminal justice client must be fully informed of who will have access to their assessments and treatment progress or lack of progress reports prior to beginning treatment. This is dissimilar to the ethical rules of psychology, social work, and professional counseling regarding confidentiality, where the assumption is that confidentiality is never violated without the client's consent. They must also be informed that if the therapist determines the client presents a danger to another, the therapist has the obligation to report such danger to the victim and the court of jurisdiction according to the Tarasoff standard (Tarasoff, 1976).

Screening

The primary purpose of screening is to identify possible problem areas that may require immediate attention such as threats of suicide or harm to others, health problems that may require attention such as the presence of high-risk factors for HIV/AIDs, STDs, hepatitis, etc, severity of the offender's criminal history, substance abuse problems, mental health problems, etc. The basic information for screening can be obtained from many sources including: (a) family members, (b)employers, (c) client self-report, (d) past correctional records, (e) past treatment records, (f) police reports, (g) arrest records, (h) drug test results from a urinalysis examination, (i) medical reports, and (j) court records.

Screening does not generally identify what kind of problem the offender may have, or how serious a problem may be if identified during the screening process. The screening process usually determines if a referred offender is eligible for services, and if further assessment is needed. Screening for eligibility is making a determination if the appropriate services are available for the offender, or if the offender needs to be referred to another agency that can better serve them. The screening process should not assign a DSM-IV diagnostic impression, but rather screens for DSM symptoms that may require further evaluation or referral.

Offender Assessment

There are a number of points within the criminal justice system at which the assessment of an individual's risk of future violent behavior is relevant (Campbell, 1995). These generally include bail determination hearings, sentencing, and appropriateness for community supervision and treatment. Assessment done by forensic counselors in community based outpatient forensic programs should focus on identifying risk factors, identifying problems amenable to treatment rather than making predictions (Deisler, 2003).

Assessment is the process of defining the details of an identified problem for the purpose of making specific treatment recommendations for treating and effectively impacting the problem. Assessments are more methodical than screenings, although their depth and scope may vary considerably according to the following factors: (a) time available to conduct the assessment, (b) training and skill of the assessor, (c) limited confidentiality, (d) availability of treatment, (e) sources of information utilized for the assessment, and (f) accuracy of the information utilized for the assessment.

All offenders are not the same, and there are special populations, which require different assessment tools, and approaches, which will be briefly discussed. However, the fundamental definition and purpose of assessment for all the offender populations remain basically the same.

Offender assessment whether adult or juvenile is the

process of collecting information through various techniques in order to determine one or more of the following: (a) problems involved in the present offense, (b) to provide a historical profile of the client, (c) to determine the presence of an offending pattern, (d) to estimate the client's risk level of re-offending, (c) to provide data for the development of a problem oriented treatment plan, (d) to determine a diagnosis, (e) to determine the prognosis for treatment, (f) to assess the client's appropriateness for treatment, (g) to identify specific types of interventions and strategies to be utilized in treatment, and possibly, (h) to provide data and recommendations to the courts. Offender assessment can simply become a ritual, which must be done as a requirement, or it can be the beginning of the rehabilitative process.

Types of Offender Assessment

There are basically four types of assessments used by most mental health professionals that specialize in treating criminal justice clients regardless of their offense which include: (a) a basic evaluation which is utilized to collect historical and current data as well as to determine the need for further psychological or psychiatric evaluation, (b) risk assessment which is utilized to identify the risk potential for the client to re-offend, program intensity and, possible requirements for special conditions, (c) treatment needs assessment to identify client treatment needs and possible strategies for the purpose of treatment planning, (d) treatment progress assessment which is utilized to determine the client's progress or lack of progress while in treatment, and treatment plan updating, and (e) recovery assessment which is utilized to assess the clients capabilities of adhering to a relapse prevention plan, abstaining from antisocial acting out behaviors, levels of change made by the client, and development of new social coping skills.

Basic Assumptions of Offender Assessment

According to many sociologists and psychologists as well as my clinical impression, criminal acting out behaviors are learned and are a choice of the individual. Those that present with a primary diagnosis of APD, sociopathy or psychopathy, the psychopathology can be viewed as a developmental disorder that is deeply rooted in their lifestyle patterns. The exceptions to this are clients that are diagnosed with an organic brain syndrome, and in many cases those diagnosed with a co-morbid psychiatric disorder. It is also generally accepted that there is no cure for APD, sociopathy or psychopathy. For the most part, criminal acting out behaviors can be broken down into a series of conscious choices according to (Samenow, 1998). It is also acknowledged that those offenders suffering from APD, sociopathy or psychopathy can learn new behaviors and adapt to a prosocial lifestyle.

Those clients referred because of sex crimes the basic assumption of assessment are similar, but also present very unambiguous differences. According to (Carich and Adkerson, 1995) offender assessment includes: (a) sexual aggression is a learned behavior which can be broken down into a series of choices at all levels of awareness, (b) offenders could also have multiple paraphilias, (c) offenders can change and monitor their own behavior, (d) sexual offending behavior is typically viewed as being developmental in nature, (e) assessment is an ongoing process, (f) offending behavior can be evaluated in patterns of recursive cycles, (g) offenders could have multiple sexual offending interests and patterns, (h) there is no acceptable cure for sexual offending problems.

It does not matter whether a client is a general offender, sex offender, or a client presenting with an alcohol or substance abuse problem, it is important that the client take responsibility for their current and past criminal behavior. When a criminal justice client appears for his first appointment prior to their assessment for intake, it is important to let them know that only clients that are guilty of their offense are seen. If they state they plead guilty to avoid a lengthy prison sentence, or they are not guilty, advise them you are referring them back to court or probation because you do not counsel innocent people. This never fails to impact the client who will reconsider very quickly that they are in fact guilty and accept responsibility. If they don't, refer them back. This cuts across a lot of resistance quickly, and makes the assessment process much easier for them and the assessor.

In over thirty years of treating criminal justice clients in my practice, I had many clients choose to take the offer to go back to probation because they were innocent. They were always referred back a week or so later accepting responsibility for their offense. The client taking responsibility for their criminal behavior and being accountable is essential in order for the assessment to be accurate, and their treatment to be effective.

Offender assessment can be viewed as a dynamic and on going process requiring excellent clinical and diagnostic skills so as to detect deception, which is designed to minimize their present and past criminal acts, as well as to overcome their resistance, and tendency to manipulate and control others. It is useful during the assessment process to separate the client from their criminal behaviors and not be overly confrontational. It is also important to recognize inconsistencies in what the client reports and what is actually in the official record. However, loud, rude, demeaning confrontation is not ethical or really required to get positive results.

An effective interviewing technique to utilize with almost all criminal justice clients that effectively defeats their resistance is Motivational Interviewing techniques developed by Miller and Rollnick 1991, which is a process for assessing the client's willingness to change, and utilizing procedures based on the client's readiness toward the probability of positive change. The view that confrontation must be used with criminal justice clients because they all possess impenetrable defense mechanisms is most likely the result of impression on the part of therapists with minimal skills in the treatment of a forensic population than as result of research. Miller and Rollnick 1991, say that the use of heavy confrontational techniques are more a result of practice than research and is not necessary for a client to be motivated to seek treatment.

Confrontation of the harsh variety has been believed to be uniquelyeffective, perhaps the only strategy for dealing with alcoholics and addicts. Yet confrontational strategies of this kind have not been supported by clinical outcome studies. Therapist behaviors associated with this approach have been shown to predict treatment failure—there is no persuasive evidence that aggressive tactics are even helpful, let alone superior or preferable strategies in the treatment of addictive behaviors or other problems.

Denial and resistance from court-referred clients should be viewed as being a normal reaction to their identified behaviors and characteristics, which have been perceived as being undesirable by others, and is now a threat to their freedom. According to Miller and Rollnick 1991, it is the behavior of the therapist that brings forth resistance and denial in the client. Again, according to Miller and Rollnick: the purpose of confrontation is to see and accept reality, so that one can change accordingly... and confrontation is a goal in many different forms of treatment for a wide variety of problems. The question is this: What are the most effective ways for helping people to examine and accept reality, particularly uncomfortable reality?

Regardless of what type of assessment you are doing, the goal is to collect accurate information given voluntarily. This is not as difficult as you may think it is, even from clients referred from the criminal justice system. Most people, even criminal justice clients, like nothing else better than to talk about themselves. The most resistant client will eventually surrender if they perceive that you are genuinely invested in them. It is for this reason that I stress the use of MI techniques, which requires genuineness, caring, and empathy. Client assessment also requires active listening, which is the key to effective communication with the client. It requires paying attention to all that the client is saying, and conveying that attention to the client both nonverbally as well as verbally. It is important to maintain good eye contact with the client, which enables you to observe and evaluate the client's responses to your questions.

During the assessment process try to utilize "what, where, when and how" questions as opposed to "why" questions. What, where, when and how are generally open ended questions which describe the process of what we are seeking and encourages the client to explore something to which they alluded, and why questions are closed, and generally begin with the word because followed with a very lengthy rationalization by the client. Open-ended questions are very effective during the assessment process and generally can't be answered with just a few short words, but rather encourages the client to share more about themselves and places the burden of speaking on the client. For example, say a juvenile indicates during the assessment that they are unhappy at home and "they want out," don't be satisfied with that statement, explore further, and say something like, "So you feel terrible about your home situation and feel trapped there. What exactly is it that you feel terrible about?" What you are doing is encouraging the client to clarify their general statement by providing more specific and concrete examples of their generalized feelings of unhappiness. By probing with open-ended questions, you may be providing the juvenile the first real opportunity to really explore and vent their feelings with regard to their home life. What's more, the client's acting out behaviors and legal problems may be a direct or indirect consequence of their home situation. Utilizing Motivational Interviewing techniques, offenders are not told what to do, but are asked what they want to do. All key questions are open ended and well timed, Miller and

Rollnick, 1991. Examples of key open-ended questions are:

- What do you think you will do?
- What does this mean about your drinking?
- It must be uncomfortable for you now, seeing all this ... What's the next step?
- What do you think has to change?
- What are your options?
- Of the things I have mentioned here, which for you are the most important reasons to change? How are you going to do it?
- What's going to happen now?
- Where do you go from here?
- How would you like things to turn out for you now, ideally?
- What concerns you about changing your lifestyle?
- What would be some of the good things about making a change?

Preparing for the Assessment

Preparing to do a client assessment regardless of the charge they were referred for requires a lot of work on part of the assessor. At the time of intake when the client is required to do their initial paperwork, the intake counselor should obtain all releases of information required so as to have the appropriate official records available for the clinician that will be responsible for the client's assessment.

Prior to assessing the client, it is important for the assessor to do their homework and become familiar with the client by thoroughly reviewing the case materials available from the following sources:

- Police reports
- Victim's statement
- Prosecutor's report
- Correctional reports and records
- Previous counseling or psychiatric reports
- Pre-sentence report (PSI)
- Arrest record
- Medical records
- Court records

On the basis of these materials you should be able to formulate the questions that you plan to ask during the assessment, and be able to address any incongruence that may arise between what the official record contains, and what the client says. Being prepared for the assessment assists in overcoming a client's initial resistance and also provides structure keeping you in control of the interview.

Professional Considerations in Assessments

Your very first contact with the client is important to the assessment outcome regardless of the crime the client committed. There must not be any indication of a condescending, or condemnatory attitude in your voice or your nonverbal behaviors. It is important that you treat the client with: (a) respect and as an individual, (b) separate the client as a person from their criminal charges and deviant behavior, (c) do not express shock or repulsion at their crime or criminal history, and (d) respect your client as a person capable of making positive change.

That first impression will certainly guide much of what will happen between you and the client during the assessment. It is imperative, then, that a positive rapport be established. Greet your client by looking them straight in the eye and offer a firm handshake and smile. Your initial statement should be something like "Good afternoon, Mr. Jones. My name is Dr. Emily Smith. I will be doing your assessment today." You have now introduced yourself and your role. The next step is to establish yourself as a professional who is knowledgeable about the client's problem.

The interview should begin by asking the client if they know and understand the purpose of the assessment. If the client indicates they don't understand, and many of them won't, then you should explain fully the purpose of the assessment. You should also explain to the client in detail of the kind of information you want to obtain, what it will be used for, who will have access to the assessment, and the limitations on confidentiality. However, do not disclose all the information you have. This places the client in a position of having to guess what you do or don't know—many times resulting in more truthful or impulsive responses. Always ask open-ended questions with what, when, where or how instead of why, pursuing any thinking errors, cognitive distortions, or defense structures revealed during the interview. Don't be naive and always believe or trust what the client is telling you. Remember, whether a client is a general offender, sexual offender, or a client referred for an alcohol or drug offense, the symptoms they all have in common are denial, minimization, deflection, rationalization, and distorting information.

Co-Occurring Disorders

It is not unusual during the assessment process to discover that a substantial number of court-referred clients have one or more co-occurring disorders in addition to their antisocial personality disorder. Much of the literature that is related to co-occurring disorders in APD criminal justice clients generally focuses on substance abuse and the more severe co-morbid psychiatric disorders (e.g., schizophrenia, bipolar disorder, and major affective disorders). However, it is not unusual to uncover during the assessment process less severe disorders such as, anxiety, attention deficit disorder (ADD), hyperactive disorder (HD), adjustment disorders, phobia disorders and post traumatic stress disorder (PTSD) which are also very common among antisocial personality disordered clients. It is important in assessing the criminal justice client to be certain to screen and assess for these disorders. Because of the high rates of co-occurring disorders among criminal justice clients, identification of one disorder should immediately trigger screening for other disorders examining the relationship of the disorders and the client's criminal acting out behaviors.

Any co-occurring disorder will definitely have an

interactive effect and cause difficulties making a primary diagnosis. When identifying a co-occurring disorder it is important to assess the interactive effects, it may have on the APD in order to establish an accurate primary diagnosis. Steps you may use to assess the interactive effects of a co-occurring disorder are as follows:

1. Assess the significance of the APD by obtaining a sequential history from the client, family, and official records describing the onset of the client's antisocial behaviors.

2. Determine whether the co-occurring disorder symptoms such as substance abuse, anxiety, PTSD, HD, depression, etc, occurred prior to or after the onset of APD symptoms. For example, if the co-occurring symptoms of depression were present prior to the onset of the APD, the APD may be the result of the client acting out of a depressive state, and should be further evaluated. If the co-occurring disorder is substance abuse, which began after the onset of the clients APD symptoms, the substance abuse may be the result of the clients APD and should be further evaluated.

Whether a disorder is primary or secondary, it will determine the prognosis and treatment approach. Both disorders also require treatment and periodic assessment in order to determine which symptoms are persistent, and which symptoms change.

Psychosocial Assessment

The beginning of the assessment and evaluation process begins with the taking of a comprehensive psychosocial history from the client. The psychosocial assessment should be an in depth study of the offender based upon a clinical interview by a mental health professional. The psychosocial assessment examines and reports on the offender's functioning within different life spheres describing the offender's mental and social state. Doing the psychosocial during a clinical interview also provides the opportunity to address incongruence between what the client is reporting and what the official record contains. Information for this assessment may be available within the official record, from family members, spouse, significant other's, employers, and the client. Prior to the assessment, it is helpful to have an interview with the client's family if they are available and cooperative in order to obtain accurate early developmental and childhood information of which the client may not be aware. Unfortunately, in the majority of cases the offender's family generally declines participation in the assessment and treatment of the offender, and is generally uncooperative. The psychosocial assessment examines the offender's functioning historically in order to identify and determine how the various historical factors have contributed to the offender's daily life functioning. At a minimum, the psychosocial assessment should contain the following demographic and identifying data:

1. *Identifying information*: name, age, date of birth, marital status, number of children, siblings, race, present residence, phone contact number, contact person in event of emergency, educational level.

2. *Reason for referral*: court/probation/attorney, and reason for referral.

3. *Presenting problem*: history of present case, any prior attempts to resolve similar problems?

4. *Observations*: physical appearance, grooming, mood, speech, cooperativeness, any unusual habits, and mental status, i.e., orientation to time, place, and person.

5. *Developmental history*: early life experiences?

6. *Educational history*: educational experiences, level of education, grades, suspensions, peer relationships, learning problems, learning disabilities, vocational interests?

7. *Social history*: significant life events, recent changes, support groups, peer relationships, values, leisure activities, and group memberships?

8. *Family history*: immediate and extended families, childhood relationship, present relationships, significant experiences?

9. *Marital history*: how long married, divorces, reason for divorces, quality of the marital relationship, arguments, infidelity, primary provider, any drinking, or drugs prior to marriage and after?

9. *Living conditions and financial support*: present place of residence, type of neighborhood, roommates, rent expense, utility expenses, and food expenses?

10. *Employment history:* types of employment, length of employments, work problems such as suspensions, wages earned, job responsibilities, terminations, absenteeism, relationships with colleagues and employers?

11. *Military history*: branch of service, length of duty, rank, dates and age of enlistment, type of discharge, offenses that have been committed while in service, any use of alcohol or drugs?

12. *Present legal issues*: description of present offense.

13. *Criminal history*: dates, ages, offenses, incarcerations, sentence lengths, any difficulties while incarcerated, any use of drugs while incarcerated, violent or nonviolent crimes, motivations to commit the crimes, any use of weapons, attitudes about committing a crime, use of alcohol or drugs prior to the crime, thoughts, feelings and behaviors prior to, during and after the crimes, type of victims, look for patterns such as committing a crime once per month, every three months, etc. If the record is severe refer for further evaluation or administer the MMPI, PAI, PCL-R or other psychological assessment tool to rule out psychopathy or mental illness.

14. *Gang history:* name of gang, gang rules, offender's rank within the gang, ages of involvement, types of gang activities, reason for joining a gang, attitude, allegiance and loyalty toward the gang, reason for leaving the gang?

15. *Alcohol history*: any alcoholism in the family, age offender first used alcohol, how often and how much did the offender drink, what kind of alcohol, beer, wine or whiskey, does the offender still drink and how often and how much, were they ever arrested for an alcohol

related offense, at what ages, for what and how often, did or does the offender drink alone or with others, how much must they drink in order to become intoxicated. Look for evidence of increase in frequency and amounts to establish tolerance. If it is determined they may be alcohol dependent or abuser administer the Michigan Alcohol Screening Test (MAST) or the SASSI. Is the offender dependent and unable abstain from drinking and in need of detoxification?

16. *Drug use history*: collect the same data as delineated above in the alcohol history, ages, type of drugs used, how often, how much, overdoses, previous treatments, current use, was drugs used in any of the past offenses, was drugs used prior to or during the present offense?

17. *Other addictions*: types of addictions, gambling, sex, nicotine, food.

18. *Medical history*: childhood diseases, present medical problems, age of last physical examination and results, dental health. Are there any indicators the offender may be in need of medical assistance or referred for a physical examination? Past and present medications?

19. *Mental health history*: previous psychological or psychiatric evaluations, ages, dates, reasons for evaluation, types of psychotropic medications past and present, previous psychiatric diagnoses, hospitalizations, where and for how long and for what, number of hospitalizations. Determine if there are any indicators

that the client may be in need of psychiatric evaluation or referral?

20. *Psychosexual history*: age at the time of the offender's first sexual experience, age client first masturbated and the frequency of masturbation, sexual preference males, females or both, was the offender ever sexually abused, has the offender ever sexually abused anyone, attitude and beliefs about sex, what are the offender's age preferences, ages and gender, does the offender have sexual fantasies about certain sexual acts, has the offender ever had a sexually transmitted disease, are they promiscuous, does the offender become easily aroused, if referred because of committing a sex offense what are the offender's victim type preferences (victimology), what are there offending patterns, how many sexual offenses did they commit, what was the relationship with the victims, family member, friend, significant other, or a stranger, was there violence before, during or after the offense, does the offender have periods of normal sexual activity, is the offender presently involved in an age appropriate relationship, does the offender need to be further evaluated by a sex offender treatment specialist?

21. *Religion*: what is the offender's religious affiliation, what is their beliefs and attitudes about religion, does the offender presently practice their religion, if not why, if yes how does the offender feel about violating their belief system?

22. *Nutritional*: eating habits, types of foods consumed, eating frequency, fast foods or home prepared, does the offender generally eat alone, with others or family members?

22. *Strengths and weaknesses*:

23. *Barriers that may affect treatment*: lack of housing, unemployment, etc.

24. *Recommendations*:

25. *Prognosis*:

26. *Multi-axis diagnostic impression:* a multi-axis DSM diagnosis should be performed with statements in all five axes as listed below:

    1. Clinical Disorders

    2. Personality Disorders; Mental Retardation

    3. General Medical Condition

    4. Psychosocial and Environmental Problems

    5. Global assessment of functioning

Alcohol and Substance Abuse Assessment

Because of the high incidence of alcohol and drug related crimes, an assessment for a substance abuse disorder should be performed on every court-referred client that includes a history of alcohol and/or drug abuse, identifying first, last and current use, as well as type, frequency and route of use. The following substance abuse disorders should be documented in the client's chart as having been assessed: alcohol, cocaine/crack, heroin, THC, and methamphetamine.

There are quite a few alcohol and substance abuse screening tools available that can be used in conjunction with the psychosocial alcohol and substance abuse information obtained during the clinical interview. All of these instruments are self-report inventories, which must be used carefully, because there is always a validity issue as you can never be certain that the client responded truthfully. A few instruments have scales to detect deceptions; however, these are generally not fool proof. Some instruments you may want to consider using will be discussed.

The Michigan Alcohol Screening Test (Selver, 1971) is a twenty-four-item inventory that is easy to administer and score, and is readily available. It is an inventory of drinking habits that takes approximately 10–15 minutes to administer. The test items are scored "0" for a non-drinking response, and depending on the test item, "1," "2," or "5" for a drinking response. The total possible score is 53. A score of 0–4 is thought to be nonalcoholic, a score of 5–6 indicates an alcohol problem, and 7–9 is considered alcoholism.

There is a very similar instrument to measure drug use, which is The Drug Abuse Screening Test (DAST) developed by (Skinner, 1982) and was derived from the Michigan Alcohol Screening Test. The scoring procedure is basically the same.

Another and more reliable instrument that can be easily administered in ten to fifteen minutes is the Substance Abuse Subtle Screening Instrument Inventory-3 (Glen Miller, 1997) generally referred to as the SASSI-3. The SASSI-3 is widely used in treatment centers, hospitals, potential employee screening, correctional facilities, and the court systems. The SASSI is very simple to score providing a profile form with females on one side, and males on the other, which is used to plot the test scores, with raw scores, which are converted to T scores. The conversion is computed for you on the profile form. However, whatever other data you have gathered on the offender's alcohol or drug use should also be considered along with the SASSI results.

Risk Assessment

Offender risk assessment is recommended for all clients referred by the criminal justice system for evaluation and treatment. However, prior to any clinical assessment, it is ethically required for the assessor to obtain informed consent from the offender and to fully explain the use of the assessment results. It is generally recommended that any client assessment as to the risk of re-offending should only be done post-adjudication, but prior to sentencing. It is not the purpose of any assessment to determine an offender's guilt or innocence; therefore, if you are requested to provide a risk assessment prior to adjudication, the ethical response would be to decline the request.

Static versus Dynamic Risk Assessment

historical/changeable

Risk assessment is important for the police, courts, correctional workers, treatment providers, and the community. Risk assessment generally answers two questions. First, how likely is this offender to re-offend? Second, how can we reduce this risk? Different types of risk factors are pertinent for different types of risk decisions. Fore example, static (historical) factors such as prior criminal history, age at first offense, number of incarcerations, treatment failures, violation of probation or parole release, all can be used to assess the offender's long-term potential to reoffend.

The evaluation of change in the offender's risk level requires the consideration of a different set of risk factors that are referred to as dynamic (changeable) risk factors that are a target for treatment such as, substance abuse, poor living environment, poor attitude, anger, unemployment, etc.

There are a number of well-researched risk assessment tools available for general offenders (Andrews and Bonta, 1998) and for sex offenders (Hanson, 1998) that identifies both static and dynamic risk factors, but it is unclear how well they are able to evaluate changes in risk level. Presently, the most accurate approach to risk assessment depends upon objective, actuarial scales. The scales detail the risk factors that should be measured as well as their importance. Assessment instruments that focus on static factors have always done well at predicting long-term recidivism for general offenders and sex offenders as well. However, these instruments are not able to measure changes in risk levels.

Research over the past thirty years has identified a number of dynamic risk factors for general recidivism such as associating with antisocial peers, poor environment, substance abuse, poor attitude, etc, which have been organized into actuarial risk scales which appear to have as much predictive accuracy as static risk factors.

Knowledge of both static and dynamic risk factors is required to effectively treat and supervise general offenders and sex offenders as well. For example, an assessment of high risk by a static risk assessment tool may suggest the need for incarceration or another type of structured environment to protect the public; however, without identifying the dynamic factors, there is no way to determine when the offender could be safely released.

Methods of Assessment

Methods of assessing the risk of violence or re-offending can be categorized as either clinical or actuarial. All the actuarial approaches to assessment require the collection of historical data pertaining to the offender, which can indicate the probability of the offender to re-offend. The risk factors measured by actuarial assessment instruments can be either static (unchangeable) or dynamic (changeable). Some examples of unchangeable static risk factors can include: (a) age at the time of offense, (b) number of arrests and convictions, (c) past failures in treatment, (d) probation or parole violations, (e) number of divorces, (f) number of incarcerations, and, (g) history of past abuse. These examples are used only to communicate that static risk factors are historical and unchangeable. An example of dynamic risk factors that are changeable which may eventually lower the offender's risk level include, but not limited to include: (a) alcohol or drug abuse, (c) anger, (d) poor attitude, (e) poor social skills, (f) poor inter-personal relationships, and (g) unemployment. Clinical assessments require clinical interviewing and are based upon the assessor's clinical judgment utilizing a more holistic approach, taking into consideration the offender's physical, mental, and social condition, not just the offender's present situation. A clinical assessment most often considers the offender's personality traits, developmental history, mental illness, biological, social, and psychological factors that may be related to offending.

No method of risk assessment is perfect and at the very best is educated guesswork, whether utilizing an actuarial or clinical approach. However, the use of both methods combined may result in a more accurate assessment of the offender's risk than just using one method alone. There are different types of risk assessment tools. Some are used to predict-general re-offending, and others are used to predict sexual re-offending. Different instruments are utilized for adolescents in both situations, general re-offending risk and sexual re-offending risk. Following will be a discussion of only adult (age eighteen or over) instruments that can be used with both types of offenders. They will be briefly discussed separately.

Sex Offender Risk Assessment
STATIC-99

The most commonly utilized static risk assessment for adult sex offenders is the Static-99 (Hanson, and Thornton). The Static-99 utilizes only static factors that have been seen in the literature to correlate with sexual reconviction in adult males. The strengths of the Static-99 are that it uses risk factors that have been empirically shown to be associated with sexual recidivism and the Static-99 gives explicit rules for combining these factors into a total risk score. With the Static-99 an interview with the offender is not necessary to score the instrument. The offender's official records may be utilized for scoring purposes because all items are historical. The Static-99 is easy to score and provides an estimate level of risk "0–1" being Low Risk, "2–3" Moderate Risk, "4–5" Moderate High Risk, and a score of "6" or higher is considered High Risk. It is strongly recommended that if the Static-99 is being considered for an assessment that the assessor be well trained and experienced in sexual offending assessment.

Vermont Assessment of Sex Offender Risk

The Vermont Assessment of Sex Offender Risk (VASOR) was originally designed to assist probation and parole agents in making placement and supervision decisions (McGrath and Hoke, 1994). The VASOR is composed of two scales, a thirteen re-offense risk scale, and a six-item violence scale. The re-offense risk scale is designed for assessing the likelihood of sexual recidivism. The violence scale is designed for assessing the nature of an individual's violence history and offense severity. The interaction of these variables, re-offense risk and violence, are considered important factors for determining an individual's overall risk level (McGrath, 1995).The procedures for scoring the VASOR are simple, but should include an interview with the offender, as well as a careful review of all the official records. The VASOR scores from the two scales are plotted on a scoring grid where the intersection falls into one of three risk categories: low, moderate, or high risk. Training is recommended and it is critical that the user of the VASOR carefully read the manual as well as having a basic understanding of risk factors related to sexual offending, recidivism and principles of psychological assessment (McGrath, 1994).

Minnesota Sex Offender Screening Tool-Revised

The Minnesota Sex Offender Screening Tool-Revised (MnSOST-R) is a 16 item psychological instrument used to maximize the predictive power of the assessment. The revised version correlates .45 with sexual recidivism and possesses extremely high true positive rates of 70%-90% on the cut scores. There is also evidence that the

MnSOST-R is capable of predicting general criminal re-offending with reasonable accuracy.

Sex Offender Needs and Progress Scale

The Sex Offender Treatment Needs and Progress Scale was designed by (Robert McGrath, and Georgia F. Cumming, 2003) to aid counselors, case workers, correctional workers, and probation and parole agents in identifying and monitoring the treatment needs, supervision needs, and progress of adult sex offenders age eighteen and older. It can be used in both residential and community settings.

The scale consists of twenty-two "dynamic" risk factors that are amenable to change and a target for intervention with sex offenders. Some examples of dynamic risk factors are: (a) alcohol or drug abuse, (b) poor attitude, (c) poor social skills, and (d) anger, (e) poor living environment, (f) poor relationships, and (g) unemployment.

The instrument is easily administered and scored; however, the user should carefully read the manual and in addition should have training that includes scoring practice cases in order to optimize scoring accuracy and reliability. The instrument is administered and scored at intake and, at six-month intervals reflecting the offender's level of functioning for the previous six months. Scoring criteria for the Sex Offender Treatment Needs and Progress Scales scoring criteria are based on the following scale: "0" minimal or no need for improvement, "1" some need for improvement, "2" considerable need for improvement, and "3" very considerable need for improvement.

Abel Assessment for Sexual Interest

The Abel Assessment for Sexual Interest is a psychological instrument developed by Dr. Gene Abel, which provides an objective measurement of deviant sexual interests. The Abel Assessment is a computer driven instrument that provides the assessor with an objective reaction time measure of deviant sexual interests. The Abel Assessment may be completed in approximately thirty minutes and shows the test taker slides of adults, teens, and children. Objective reaction time measuring twenty-two sexual areas are compared utilizing "Z" scores and self-report. A paper and pencil questionnaire is coupled with the computerized test in order to provide extensive details of the offender's history of sexual interest, degree of control, accusations, and other information. The instrument assesses most dangerous clients, least dangerous clients, and clients most likely to commit a sex crime.

All of the above instruments with the exception of the Abel Assessment for Sexual Interest can be down loaded free from the Community Sex Offender Management web site at www.csom.org.

General Offender Risk Assessment

Empirically based violence and re-offending prediction instruments that are-available for assessing general offenders are presented below. It should be noted that the majority of instruments available for both sex offenders and general offenders alike are far from being perfect predictions in terms of their sensitivity (e.g., percentage of true positives) and specificity (i.e., percentage of true negatives). Therefore, the use of multiple measures to predict violence or probable re-offending is recommended. I personally do not endorse or recommend the use of any particular risk assessment instrument. Presented below are a few instruments you may want to consider utilizing in your risk assessment of general offenders.

Psychopathy Checklist List - Revised (PCL-R)

The Psychopathy Checklist-Revised (PCL-R) developed by (Hare, 1991) is a clinical rating scale of twenty items used to assess the degree to which an offender has characteristics of psychopathy. All of the items in the instrument are scored on a three-point scale according to a specific decisive factor gathered from the offender's official records, and a semi- structured interview. A score of "0" is given if an item does not apply, "1" if it somewhat applies, and "2" if it fully applies. The PCL-R assesses lifestyle, criminal behavior, glib and superficial charm, grandiosity, pathological lying, need for stimulation, conning and manipulating, poor behavioral controls, lack of remorse, callousness, irresponsibility, impulsivity, and failure to accept responsibility. The scaled scores are utilized to predict the risk of re-offense.

Users of the PCL-R should possess an advanced degree and be a licensed mental health professional having had training and experience with forensic populations. The PCL-R can be obtained through the publisher Multi-HealthSystems www.mhs.com.

Minnesota Multi-Phasic Personality Inventory - 2

The MMPI-2 is a psychological instrument that was originally developed by (Starke R. Hathaway, et al. 1942) that can be used to assess the presence of psychopathy and other psychopathologies. The MMPI-2 is a self-administered examination that consists of 567 items. There are ten major scales, four validity measures and several extra measures, which mostly deal with psychiatric, psychological, neurological, and physical symptoms. The MMPI-2 is widely used in criminal justice, correctional, community forensic facilities, hospitals, and community based outpatient facilities. The MMPI-2 has direct significance to forensic applications and the ability to determine the presence of various symptoms of psychopathology.

Historical, Clinical, Risk Management (HCR-20)

Another useful instrument for risk management is the Historical, Clinical, Risk Management - HCR-20 (Webster, et al, 1997). The HCR-20 assists assessors to determine the best management strategies for potentially violent offenders, mental health patients, and others. An example would be if an offender were referred for an assessment prior to their sentencing in order for the court to determine the potential for violence, how the court should proceed in the case, and what kind of facility or treatment the offender may require.

The HCR-20 consists of twenty probing questions within three main domain areas: historical, clinical, and risk management. The domains are coded and scored with a rating of "0" not present, "1" possible/less serious, and "3" definite/serious. The historical domain of the instrument covers ten areas: (a) previous violence, (b) age at first offense, (c) relationship instability, (d) employment problems, (e) substance use problems, (f) major mental illness, (g) psychopathy, (h) early life mal-adjustment, (i) personality disorders, (j) past supervision or treatment failure.

Adult Re-offense Risk Assessment

The Adult Re-offense Risk Assessment - (ARRA) was developed by (Deisler, 2004) for adult general offenders age 18 and over. It was specifically designed to assist clinical staff and criminal justice personnel in making treatment decisions and intensity of supervision needs.

The ARRA is composed of twenty-two items, four-teen static risk factors, and eight dynamic risk factors that are considered important for determining an offender's overall risk of re-offending. The ARRA is not an actu-arial instrument. Empirically guided clinical judgment was used to assign weights to each scale item based upon their severity and importance in predicting re-offend-ing. The ARRA demonstrated significant correlations with self-reported criminal history variables including number of violent and non-violent offenses, number of arrests and incarcerations. The ARRA also was signifi-cantly related to numerous self-reported criminal, famil-ial, and substance abuse history variables associated with offending behaviors.

The ARRA is administered by an assessor who is familiar with the case file during a clinical interview, and can be completed in 45 minutes. Each item is assigned a score of 1, 2, or 3. If there is no evidence available to score the item or it does not apply, it is scored 0. A score of 1–15 is considered Low Risk, a score of 16–20 is con-sidered Moderate Risk, and a score of 21+ is considered High Risk.

The ARRA can be down loaded free from the National Association of Forensic Counselors' web site at www.nationalafc.com.

Pros and Cons of Assessment Instruments

Screening and assessment instruments can be a very effective way of gathering client information. Most instruments are easy to use and score, and generally require limited training for their administration and scoring. Instruments that have been well researched, on the other hand, provide a level of reliability and a valid cut score.

The disadvantages of most screening and assessment instruments is that most instruments are self report questionnaires, and many times they are the only component of the screening or assessment procedure, which does not provide the opportunity to connect with your client. Without making a connection with the client, it makes it more difficult to determine if the client was honest in their response to the questionnaires. Furthermore, without making a connection with the client also rules out any opportunity to motivate the client to accept any referral for further assessment or treatment. It is best practice to have a clinical interview with the client and their family if available as part of the screening, or assessment processing addition to the use of screening, or assessment instruments.

The Importance of Accurate Assessments

An accurate assessment is extremely important for many reasons. Many times the referring court or probation department will use assessment results in their decision to either sentence the defendant to prison, or to place them on probation if the assessment indicates they are appropriate for community supervision. The assessment will also assist in the level of supervision the offender will need if placed on community supervision as well as for the need of any special conditions.

An accurate assessment also assists in treatment by identifying the offender's high-risk factors for re-offending, and the intensity of treatment that will be needed. The assessment also identifies problems to be addressed on the treatment plan and in case management.

Treatment Benefits of Providing Treatment to Offenders

Providing treatment to criminal justice clients makes good common sense and is also good public policy because it can reduce recidivism. All the available research clearly indicates that punishment alone is unlikely to have an effect on changing criminal behavior. Criminal justice clients with alcohol or drug problems co-occurring with an antisocial personality disorder are most likely to re-offend and be a danger to the community. According to the U.S. Department of Justice, 1992, half (50%) of those persons convicted of a crime were under the influence of drugs or alcohol at the time of the offense. Fifty-three percent were on probation, parole, or pre-trial release at the time of their arrest. Four out of ten had a current or past sentence for a violent offense. Thirty-nine percent had served three or more prior sentences to incarceration or probation. The identified risk factors that would be amenable to treatment that may reduce recidivism for this population included: (a) approximately thirty-one percent had grown up with a parent or guardian who abused alcohol or drugs, (b) approximately twelve percent had lived in foster homes or institution, (c) forty-six percent had a family member who had been incarcerated, (d) more than fifty percent of convicted and incarcerated women reported that they had been physically or sexually abused in the past, (e) among violent offenders, forty-one percent of those on probation, forty percent in local jails, and thirty-eight percent of those in state prison had been drinking when they committed the crime, and (f) of released sex offenders who allegedly committed another sex crime, forty percent perpetrated a new offense within a year or less from their prison discharge.

The purpose of treatment for all offenders regardless of their charge is two fold: (1) to return a productive individual, free of addictions, deviant sexual behaviors, antisocial beliefs and attitudes, back to their community equipped to live a pro-social lifestyle, and (2) to reduce the expense of crime to society. These two reasons on their own make sense and are good public policy.

Problem Oriented Treatment Planning

Treatment planning requires that the clinician address any mental health, substance abuse, and the offender's criminal behavior, each in the context of the other identified disorders. The screening and assessment results should provide information that will also be incorporated in the treatment planning process, which assisted in making preliminary decisions regarding what type of service the offender requires, as well as treatment setting, and treatment intensity.

Treatment begins with the development of a treatment plan. The treatment plan is a powerful therapeutic tool, because it is a road map that describes where the offender is, and where they will be if they follow the plans directions. I always recommend the development and use of a problem oriented treatment plan, especially in the treatment of criminal justice clients. The use of a problem oriented treatment plan lists the offender's strengths and weaknesses as well as their problems, with very specific objectives to reach the goal of solving the problem. The problem oriented treatment plan is also a very effective tool to measure the offender's progress or lack of progress while in treatment.

When there has been an accurate identification of the client's life problems that may be contributing to their criminal acting out and lifestyle, the treatment plan is developed. It is extremely important that the client and their therapist agree with each other in identifying problems. It has been an unfortunate practice, especially with criminal justice clients not to include the client in the development of the treatment plan. For the most part this practice really makes no sense because what the therapist identifies as a problem may not be what the client thinks the problem is. Treatment planning with the client participating in the process consists of the following components:

1. *Treatment plan negotiations.* This is the process of identifying and agreeing on problems, establishing the goal to solve the problem, and objectives to reach the goal.

2. *Treatment plan provisions* to fulfill the treatment plan.

3. *Treatment plan performance.* Agreement between the therapist and client on how, where and when each objective will be completed.

4. *Treatment plan completion.* Establishing the criteria for ending treatment.

5. *Treatment plan confirmation.* Developing a relapse prevention plan and a structured after-care program. A problem oriented treatment plan may have as many problems listed that may be required. Each problem may have as many objectives as may be needed to resolve each individual problem.

Following is a short example of a treatment plan:

Problem Oriented Treatment Plan

Client name: _____

Address:_____

State: _____ City: _____Zip: _____

Phone: _____ Age: _____

Date of birth: _____Marital status: _____

Number of children: _____

Ages: _____

Employment:_____

Phone: _____

Emergency contact:_____

Phone: _____

Religious affiliation: _____

Date of intake: _____

Intake counselor:_____

Present offense(s):_____

Referral source: _____

Probation/parole agent:_____

Phone:_____

Client Problems:

    1. Client lacks social control

    2. Client lacks vocational skills

Client Strengths:

    1. Client is physically healthy

    2. Client motivated to change

Problem #1: Client agrees that he suffers from a severe lack of social control as is evidenced by numerous arrests, incarcerations, probation violations, and fights resulting in his present situation.

    Goal: Client will develop awareness of his attitudes and antisocial lifestyle contributing to his lack of social control.

Objectives

1. On or before July 3, 2008, client will in group therapy share with other group members how he believes his lack of social control has created problems in his life, in relationships, and in his community. Client will ask group members for feedback.

2. On or before July 15, 2008, client will explore with his primary counselor how he believes his father abandoning him and his mother at his age 6 has contributed to his antisocial attitude and lack of social control.

As you have probably noticed, each objective specified a date, where *group therapy*, and how *sharing with group members*, to complete each objective. This is important because most offenders need a structure letting them know exactly what is to be done, what is expected of them, and when. This type of treatment plan format makes it almost impossible for the criminal justice client to go un-noticed when not fulfilling their treatment plan requirements. It also assists the therapist and treatment team to immediately identify if the client is not interested in their recovery, or if the client is preoccupied with their external life, allowing the treatment team an opportunity for early intervention and determination as to how best to approach the client's lack of progress.

As each objective is completed, it must be reflected in the client's medical record. Accurate progress notes are essential and don't have to be lengthy and burdensome. An easy system for charting progress notes that are accurate and short is the DAP system as shown below:

DATA: Mr. Smith was seen in group on July 3, 2008, at which time he worked on problem #1, objective 1. Mr. Smith shared with his group members and therapist ways he believes his lack of social control has caused him emotional, psychological, relationship, financial, and employment problems. He also shared how his self-created problems have also a burden on his family, others, and the community.

ASSESSMENT: Mr. Smith was very thorough in identifying how his lack of social control has affected his life, others, and his community. It appears that Mr. Smith spent quite a bit of time examining his past antisocial behaviors and its effects. He appeared to be remorseful during his group presentation becoming tearful and taking time to regain his composure. Mr. Smith is progressing well at this time.

PLAN: Mr. Smith will continue to be seen in group therapy twice weekly. No new problems have been identified during this session indicating any need to update his present treatment plan.

Initial Treatment Plan Focus

Problems delineated within the initial treatment plan should have been identified during the assessment process. However, once the client begins treatment and new problems are identified, the treatment plan should be updated to address the newly identified problems. Some of the issues that may be a focus of the clients' treatment plan may be: (a) financial problems, (b) the client's criminal behavior, (c) developmental issues, (d) self-esteem and identity, (e) interpersonal relationships, (f) physical or sexual abuse trauma, (g) substance abuse, (h) co-morbid psychiatric disorder, (i) family problems, (j) educational or vocational needs, (k) anger issues, (1) family reunification, (j) the clients patterns of criminality, and (k) criminal thinking.

Motivation to Fulfill Treatment Plan Goals

Most criminal justice clients don't have a lot of motivation to follow through with their treatment plans for many reasons which may include: (a) the belief that because their treatment is mandated by the court, it is further punishment, (b) hostility toward the criminal justice system which has had an impact on their lives, (c) a belief that their life situation will never change, (d) a history of failure in other treatment programs, and (d) a belief that treatment is only for mentally ill persons.

Motivating the client to fulfill treatment plan objectives and goals is the very first step in treating criminal justice clients regardless of the offense they are charged with. Without motivation to fulfill the treatment plan goals, resistance and eventual failure are certain to follow. As discussed in chapter two, Motivational Interviewing techniques are effective for increasing client motivation. To further avoid failure and reduce resistance, the objectives for each of the goals within the treatment plan should build small opportunities for the client to experience success, so the client can gain confidence in their ability to fulfill the treatment plan goals, thereby creating hope that their life situation can indeed change.

Cooperation between the referring criminal justice system and the treatment agency through collaboration can increase the client's chances for success in fulfilling their treatment plan requirements. Both agencies can effectively work together in encouraging and guiding the criminal justice client through their treatment plan and program through the use of incentives and sanctions. However, it has been my experience that in order for this partnership to work smoothly, a memorandum of understanding is necessary. The memorandum of understanding should clearly delineate each agency: (a) expectations (b) obligations (c) roles. The memo should also define: (a) what information will be reported, (b) how often it is to be reported, (c) what would be considered a violation of probation or parole, (d) what would be considered a program violation, (e) what incentives and sanctions will be utilized and under what circumstances,

(f) under what circumstances the client would be unsuccessfully terminated from treatment, (g) if the clients supervising probation or parole agent will participate in team meetings, and, (h) the specific roles of each agency in the client's treatment.

Case Management Services

The purpose of case management is to coordinate services and systems in order to connect the offender with appropriate resources while in treatment, to track progress or lack of progress, reporting information to the treatment team, and monitoring the conditions required by the courts, probation or parole authorities. Case management tasks generally include the following type of activities:

1. Assessing the offender's needs and motivation to remain crime free.

2. Communicating with the offender's probation or parole agent.

3. Identifying treatment and other services for the offender.

4. Supporting the client and assisting with other involve systems such as welfare, courts, and treatment agencies.

5. Reporting progress or lack of to other team members.

6. Monitoring on-going assessment reports

7. Monitoring chemical testing results for alcohol or drug abuse.

8. Monitoring treatment plan progress or lack of progress.

9.   Identification of essential aftercare services for continuing recovery.

It is not unusual for criminal justice clients needing assistance in finding employment or housing. Most offenders present with a long history of unemployment or job instability make financial resources minimal or non-existent. Many lack a high school education or vocational training. Assisting the offender in obtaining a general equivalency diploma (GED) and vocational training improves their likelihood of obtaining employment, and lowers the risk of re-offending. Other important case management activities may also include teaching the client basic life skills like budgeting, saving, maintaining a checkbook, filling out employment applications, providing job seeking skill classes, and parenting classes which all assist in lowering the risk of recidivism.

The case manager in most treatment facilities providing services to offenders is generally the primary therapist, who must work together with the court, probation, or parole agent in order for treatment to be most effective, and to also ensure the offender is complying with their treatment and remaining crime free. This partnership between the case manager and the referral source shares the responsibility of treatment continuity and offender accountability across both systems.

Duration of Treatment

The duration of treatment should be determined by the results of the assessment, as well as a careful assessment of the length and severity of the offender's criminal acting out behaviors. The therapist should keep in mind at all times, that there are no short-term solutions to long-term unrelenting problems when determining intensity and duration of treatment.

All criminal justice clients with a substance abuse disorder, sex offender, or general offenders with anti-social personality disorder or sociopathy are chronic re-offenders. The problem oriented treatment plan must be of suitable intensity and length to be effective. There are no short-term solutions for these clients' long-term problems. The longer the duration of treatment up to one to two years, the more positive the treatment outcome. The longer and more inclusive the treatment regimen is, the probability that the offender regardless of the nature of their offense will be alcohol free, drug free, arrest free, and criminal justice free in the future. Treatment outcome always improves when the course of treatment is longer, followed up with an effective aftercare program.

Client Treatment Matching

There exists a diversity of treatment approaches and treatment settings in which general criminal offenders, offenders with substance abuse problems, and sex offenders may be treated. However, recent criminal justice referral trends have been leaning more and more toward community based type programs for offenders because of prison overcrowding as these programs become available. Criminal justice alternatives to incarceration have included diversion programs, pretrial release programs with a condition the offender enter into treatment, and provisional probation with specific conditions. Research has consistently shown that combining criminal justice sanctions with treatment can be effective in reducing recidivism. Treatment for criminal justice involved offenders may be delivered prior to, during, after, or in lieu of incarceration. Whatever treatment setting the client is eventually placed, the setting must meet the client's treatment needs and provide the best opportunity for a successful recovery from their criminal lifestyle. Discussed are the treatment settings most commonly utilized for offender treatment that have proven successful in reducing general re-offending, sexual re-offending, and substance abuse recovery.

TREATMENT MODELS

There are several models of treatment that are offender and offense specific. The central treatment model utilizes a multi-disciplinary approach, which includes a medical staff, psychiatric staff, psychological staff, social work staff, and is generally utilized in state or federal hospital based programs, or long-term residential programs.

The cognitive-behavioral model is the most commonly utilized in the treatment of offenders, which utilizes cognitive restructuring techniques, and behavioral techniques in addressing the offender's criminal behaviors and life problems. This model is very effective in addressing the offender's social functioning deficits and learning how to maintain social control. Most cognitive-behavioral offender programs provide individual, group, and family therapy, as well as psycho-educational classes. The program focus is on social control and relapse prevention.

The psychosocial model is not as effective as the cognitive-behavioral model because it is dependent upon the use of peer groups, educational classes, and focus groups, which for most offenders does not assist in the resolution of their life problems through therapy.

Basic Principles of Offender Treatment

Criminal behavior is both a criminal justice and mental health issue. Trained therapists that work with offender populations know, that the majority of criminal justice clients seen have other problems that are directly linked to their criminal acting out behavior. Some of the more common problems that are directly linked to criminal behaviors include: (a) sexual addiction in the case of many sexual offenses, (b) personality disorders, (c) developmental interferences, (d) neurological disorder, (e) anger/rage issues, (f) alcohol abuse, (g) substance abuse, (h) family dysfunction, (i) poverty, (j) poor living environment, and (k) lack of educational/vocational training. Although none of these disorders and problems excuses the offender's criminal acts, they contribute to their happening.

In the offender treatment field, it is accepted that there is no cure for anti-social personality disorder, alcohol dependence, substance abuse dependence, or sexual assault; however, it is also accepted that such clients can recover and live pro-social life styles. Recovery and living a pro-social lifestyle requires that the offender must take responsibility for their present offense and discuss in treatment any previous crimes they may have committed. Treatment helps only those offenders who acknowledge their problems and are motivated to change. It requires that the offender comply with treatment, fulfill their treatment plan goals and objectives, and be accountable.

It is also accepted that group therapy with a male and female co-therapist is best practice; however, it is also acknowledged that not all offenders are appropriate for group therapy. Cognitive-behavioral therapy is also considered to be best practice in cognitive restructuring of the clients cognitive distortions.

The basic premise and goal of offender treatment is the prevention of criminal behavior through the means of high quality treatment, and the protection of the public through effective offender management. Through training and continuing education, continued development of high practice standards in the offender treatment field. The overall goal of offender treatment is to return to the community a recovering offender that is prepared to live a pro-social lifestyle.

Therapeutic Communities

Therapeutic Communities (TC's) provide care in a non-hospital setting twenty-four hours per day with planned lengths of stay of six to twelve months or longer. The TC model focuses on the re-socialization of the offender utilizing the program's entire community of resident's, staff, and social environment as dynamic components in the resident's treatment, and in creating a total learning environment. General criminal offending, addiction, or sexual offending is viewed within the framework of the offender's social and psychological deficits. Treatment focus within the TC is on the offender becoming accountable, responsible, and developing a pro-social lifestyle and attitudes. The TC environment is tightly structured, and may or may not utilize heavy confrontational techniques. TC activities are designed to assist residents in exploring their belief system, self-concept, offending patterns, social skills deficits, and developing new skills to more effectively interact with others.

Intensive Outpatient Treatment

Intensive outpatient treatment is generally a tightly structured program very similar to a residential program with planned lengths of participation of six to eighteen months. Most intensive outpatient programs are based on positive and negative reinforcement. Intensive outpatient programs provide multi-levels of intensity based upon the offender's needs and risk level. For example, the offender may be assigned to a level four program, which requires they participate in therapy four times per week up to three hours per session. As the offender progresses in treatment, they are rewarded by being lowered to a level three program requiring they participate three times per week up to three hours per session. As the offender continues to progress they are eventually lowered to a level two program requiring they participate twice weekly up to two hours per session, and eventually to level 1 at which time they are only required to be seen once per week for one hour sessions. If treatment progress stops, or if the offender begins to show signs of slipping back into their previous thinking patterns and behavior attitudes, they are reassigned back to level four. This process of positive and negative reinforcement may continue until the offender becomes consistent in their treatment and recovery from general criminal offending, sexual offending, or addiction. Intensive outpatient programs can be comparable to residential programs in the services they provide, and in effectiveness depending upon the offender's needs, and severity of their problems. Other services available in intensive outpatient programs include psycho-educational classes, individual therapy, family and marital therapy, and urinalysis monitoring.

Traditional Outpatient Treatment

Traditional outpatient treatment is less intense, and less expensive than residential and intensive outpatient programs. Outpatient treatment is often more suitable for those offenders who have family responsibilities, extensive pro-social supports, are gainfully employed, and are at low risk of re-offending. Low intensity outpatient programs generally offer psycho-educational classes, individual, family, group therapy, and urinalysis monitoring services. Many traditional outpatient programs are designed to treat offenders who have a co-morbid psychiatric disorder in addition to their antisocial personality disorder, sexual disorder, or drug disorder.

Community Supervised Activity Programs

These types of programs may be part of the criminal justice system or contracted outside the system by local agencies providing offender services. The type of services these programs generally provide are alcohol and drug testing and monitoring, support groups, educational services, vocational and/or skills training, employment assistance, day reporting, and aftercare services.

Halfway House

Halfway houses are transitional facilities where the client resides after being referred from a jail, prison, hospital, or outpatient program for continued support in reentering the community while the client is involved in school, vocational training, or employment. Clients are generally required to participate in therapeutic activities while they are residents such as group, individual, family, support groups, or couples therapy. Halfway houses may be private, part of an agency's services, or attached to a local jail.

Prison-Based Programs

Prison based programs for general offenders, sex offenders, and substance abusers are generally in a therapeutic community type environment. The program is separated from the general population in order to avoid any harassment from other inmates in the general population. Services provided in a prison based TC program can include substance abuse, sex offender, and general offender psycho-educational classes, group therapy, individual therapy, social skills training, and support group attendance. Most prison-based programs do not provide family or marital therapy, and if they do, it is extremely limited.

I have been a critical opponent of prison-based programs as they presently are. Very few prison-based programs have a continuum of care component attached to them once the offender is released back into the community. I have always alleged that such negligence on part of the system has been, and is a "set up" for the offender to fail. This is like sending a newly recovering alcoholic back into an alcoholic family, or an ex-gang member back to their gang. As a result, there is a high rate of relapse and re-offending attached to prison based programs.

Self Help Programs

In addition to treatment, participation in a twelve-step program should be encouraged because they provide peer support for remaining abstinent from substances, criminal activities, and coping with daily life difficulties. When offenders participate in such programs as Alcoholics Anonymous (AA), Narcotics Anonymous (NA), and Offenders Anonymous (OA) during their treatment have a non-threatening source of support in the community where they can talk openly and honestly about the challenges, barriers, confusion and turmoil of recovery.

Offenders Anonymous is a developing organization of successfully recovering ex-offenders that encourages accountability, concern for others, community involvement, and pro-social lifestyles. Offenders' Anonymous membership consists of ex-offenders without an addiction disorder whose life problems and criminal behaviors were a result of their antisocial behaviors and lifestyles. One of the OA requirements is that ex-offenders do not share the types of crimes they committed. Offenders Anonymous believes a crime is a crime regardless of its nature, which makes it a safe place for all types of offenders including sexual abusers.

CLINICAL ISSUES IN TREATMENT

Forensic Counseling and offender treatment differs from traditional counseling and treatment in that community safety always takes precedence over the offender. Forensic counseling acknowledges that there is no cure for criminal offending, and that all recovering offenders remain at risk for ten to twenty years regardless of the nature of their past crimes.

Treatment requires that the offender take responsibility not only for their present offense, but also for all their past criminal behavior and criminal lifestyle. During the treatment process, emphasis is placed on identifying the offenders cognitive distortions and restructuring them, developing interpersonal skills, understanding the harm they caused themselves, the victim, their family, and the community, identifying risk factors that contribute to their criminal acting out, identifying their cycle or pattern of criminal offending, developing social skills, developing empathy, social control, developing a pro-social support system, and the development of a relapse prevention plan. This is no easy task even for the best-trained and experienced therapist. Addressing these issues in treatment is a long hard pull, which requires that the offender be in treatment for a minimum of one to three years. Why so long? My clinical experience in treating this population exclusively for over twenty-five years, is that their are no short-term solutions to these client's long-term problems, and that any time less than that required to do the job thoroughly will result in the client re-offending. It is for this reason that it is essential to have the complete cooperation of the sentencing court and supervising probation agent, all working together in concert toward the same goal, the client's recovery.

There are many similarities in offender needs for those in the criminal justice system regardless of their offense. The general offender, sex offender, and substance abuse offender all share similar characteristics and stressors, including their uncertain legal situation. Some of their more common characteristics include criminal values, criminal thinking, rigid denial systems, and resistance to treatment efforts. They also share long histories of psychosocial and interpersonal difficulties, managing anger and stress, lack of education and vocational skills, and problems finding and maintaining gainful employment (Belenko and Peugh 1998).

This chapter addresses many of the clinical issues involved in offender treatment such as the cognitive restructuring of thinking errors, criminal thinking, anger, emotions, social skills training, denial, resistance, criminality, abandonment, attachment issues, barriers to recovery, and client basic needs.

Basic Needs

It makes no sense in attempting to assess and treat a criminal justice client who is not getting their basic life needs met such as housing, food and clothing. These clients don't benefit from treatment because all of their energy is focused on survival, not getting well. The very first step when such a client is referred is to immediately direct them into a program that will meet their basic needs. Most communities have something available such as the Salvation Army for shelter and clothing, missions, church programs, or halfway houses. Assessment of problems and risk, and treatment, should be postponed until the client is stable.

The criminal justice client's basic needs may vary depending upon their diagnosis, offense, present legal status, culture, age, gender, intellectual functioning, and availability of services designed to meet the need. Many offenders are homeless either because of having been incarcerated and released, or their behavior has become so intolerable family members don't want them living at home. Many offenders commit crimes so they will go to jail where they have a place to sleep, eat, and the availability of some medical care. For many of these offenders who may have been living on the streets, jail may be the safest environment they have been in for some time. Many become so accustomed to living on the streets, they need to be placed in a residential program that will assist them in relearning how to live in a normal and safe environment. The community based outpatient forensic program the homeless offender is referred to should have in place a plan or resources to provide these offenders with housing before being placed in treatment.

Addressing the Clients Criminality
The focus of treatment for criminal justice clients must

be offense specific with a focus on their criminality. (Antonowicz and Ross, 1994) address the need to prioritize treatment according to the criminogenic needs of criminal justice clients, particularly the specific issues that brought the client to the attention of the criminal justice system originally. These are most often the client's antisocial personality disorder, substance abuse, criminal thinking, and values. There are a variety of factors that are associated with criminal behavior, including personality disorders, substance abuse, lack of social skills, poor impulse control, impaired moral reasoning, and cognitive distortions (Wanberg and Milkman, 1998). The client's criminal thinking is particularly important to address, because clients with deep-rooted criminal lifestyles make use of cognitive distortions, which are maladaptive coping strategies to other life issues, and are not a stable risk factor of their personality.

Most offenders that are antisocial personality disorders or substance abusers have developed a street identity based upon the environmental culture in which they were raised or involved. Many offenders that have developed a street identity generally think of themselves as criminals or gangsters. This is generally in part a result of peer pressure and interactions with peers who have also accepted the traits of being a criminal. The offender's criminal identity can create a number of problems in treatment. The criminal identity of an offender is a barrier to their recovery and should be confronted in treatment. Those who have personalized a criminal identity need to learn new ways of thinking about who they really are, and to develop a more pro-social identity that is consistent with community values.

The offender's race and cultural background plays an important role in their street identity. The dynamics of race and culture are particularly obvious in the offender's environment where a number of subcultures in the form of gangs can generally be found among Caucasians, African-Americans, Asians, and Latinos. Gang affiliation reinforces the offender's criminal identity, and more often than not influences with whom the offender is able to socialize. Treatment has to take into account this characteristic of the offender's criminal identity and criminality.

There is definitely a pecking order among those who commit crimes with the child molester at the bottom of the heap. Most offenders have attained a reputation on the streets, which requires the use of a set of skills and behaviors different from the community at large. It can be a deterrent in treatment if the offender thinks they may lose their reputation or status because they are in treatment. This is particularly true with gang members because gangs are hierarchical subcultures. The therapist should be aware if the offender had a high street status or large illegal income as a result of their criminality, and may have to deal with, in treatment, the temptation of returning to their high-paying criminal occupation.

Those offenders that have been charged or convicted of a sexual offense must be isolated from the general offender while in treatment, and should be in a program that is sex offender specific, with trained sex-offender treatment specialists. Sex offenders can benefit from therapy; however, they may require more direct supervision to prevent re-offending.

Most offenders also have a tendency to have a shared

value system which includes a refusal to cooperate, being manipulative, not to confront negative behaviors by others, and to make fools of others, that is part of their criminal thinking which are maladaptive coping strategies to sabotage treatment and to maintain their dysfunctional frames of reference and should be confronted by the therapist. Many times the reluctance to cooperate and participate fully in treatment is a fear of being labeled as being "weak," "punk," or "snitch." The therapist should remain aware at all times if this dynamic is at work and confront it immediately in order to avoid a client being stigmatized as such.

Denial

Offenders almost always present with high levels of denial not found in other populations, which is a product of their criminal thinking and cognitive distortions. Many times the therapist will discover that some offenders sincerely do not believe they have committed a criminal offense, or what they have done is immoral. Denial is the most archaic of the defense mechanisms, which requires patience and skills on part of the therapist to work through successfully. Denial is persistent, especially when it involves admitting to a criminal offense or the use of drugs. Denial is also a minimization of the offender's life problems, which also utilizes rationalizations and justifications designed to protect the offender from the consequences of their behavior.

Denial must be worked through systematically for each and every problem in order to prevent it from re-occurring. During the course of my career working with offenders, I have developed a systematic model for working through the denial of all problems presented which is a modification of the Discounting Model developed by (Jacqui Schiff, 1975) for use with schizophrenics. This model recognizes the four levels of denial that must be worked through as follows:

Level 1. Denial of the existence of the problem.

Level 2. Denial of the severity of the problem.
       a)   on self
       b)   family
       c)   victims
       d)   community

Level 3. Denial of the solvability of the problem.

Level 4. Denial of one's ability to follow through with the solution of a problem.

It is never acceptable to just accept the offender's admission that committing a crime and going to jail or prison is a problem. They must also stop denying on all four levels in order to successfully extinguish denial, and to prevent re-occurrence of the same problem. Denial at any one of these four levels denies the other three levels. For example, a client denying being arrested and incarcerated is a problem is denying the existence of their problem as well as its severity, solvability and their ability to do something differently in the future. All four levels of denial are beyond the offender's awareness and distort their perception of reality. The distortion of reality works to reinforce their contaminated frame of reference, cognitive distortions and criminal life styles.

Therapeutic interventions designed to work through the offender's denial system should be well planned so as not to start below level 1. If the intervention begins below level 1, the intervention will be ineffective and result in further failure. By systematically working through the offender's denial system in sequence, it allows the offender to clearly define their problem as well as the options to solve them and to act on them.

Resistance

Resistance is not necessarily a terrible thing that will hinder progress and recovery in treatment. The offender's resistance can be viewed as their fear of facing the consequence of their criminal activities as well as their fear of their ability to comply with treatment or to make life changes. If you can understand a resistant offender's behavior as being symptomatic of their fears, you will have a way of working with their resistance. The offender's resistance should provide an opportunity for exploration that may reveal other symptoms or even clues about their interpersonal styles within the community they reside. In other words, resistance on part of the offender does not need to be interpreted as something negative, which will make it difficult for you to treat them effectively. It is way too easy to terminate an offender as a resistant client, which has a tendency to reinforce their behavior. (Ormont, 1988) associates resistance with a fear of intimacy. The underlying fear is generally of getting close to others and the vulnerability it entails.

Resistance by the criminal justice client can take many forms such as hostility, which is really very difficult to work with in a group setting because the client expressing it often does so indirectly. They may use sarcasm, jokes, scornful remarks, or not participate in group activities, no show no calls, coming to sessions late, acting bored, rolling their eyes, etc. One of the ways I deal with these types of behaviors is I have the group members one at a time tell how they are being affected and held back by the resistant client, and what they would like the client to do differently. Many times this works and sometimes it doesn't. Many times the hostile behaviors being observed may be a symptom of the client's fear of getting close to or trusting others. If the client is extremely resistant and hostile, and all interventions have failed, the client just may not be a good candidate for group therapy because they will have a negative effect on the group climate, making it difficult for others to allow themselves to be vulnerable.

Another passive aggressive maneuver a client may use to express their hostility is by replying to every intervention with "I don't know." Some simple responses you may want to try that may assist the client to get past their resistance, which is working, with the resistance, rather than against it are as follows:

Client: I don't know

Therapist: If you did know, what would you say? Let's pretend that you do know. What do you know?Say the very first thing that comes to mind. What else don't you know?

Client: I hate this place and don't want to be here.

Therapist: Who made you come here? Well, you are here. How can you make the best of it? What is hateful about being here? Where would you rather be instead?

Client: I'm afraid to talk about my past crimes in here.

Therapist: What do you fear will happen? What do you think will happen if you do? What needs to happen for you to stop being scared? What has to happen for you to feel safe in here?

Well thought out interventions and responses such as these will generally assist the client in getting past their resistance. And then again, no matter how well designed your interventions may be, some clients will still not respond positively.

Lack of Empathy

No one is born with empathy. In childhood, we learn how to respect other people and their feelings. Empathy is defined as having the ability to identify ourselves with others, and the capacity to experience sensations, thoughts, feelings, and emotions similar to those experienced by others. This is learned in childhood which most of us have been fortunate to accomplish. We first learned to love, care, and respect ourselves, which is a necessity before we can love, care, or respect others. If we do not learn and achieve these values, then we cannot share with others that which we don't have or understand ourselves. The lack of emotional integration during their early development for most personality disorders has resulted in a lack of empathy and caring for others, which is a challenging issue in the treatment of criminal justice clients with a personality disorder especially APD.

Empathy is a skill that can be taught; however, it entails a different kind of learning that will not be achieved through psycho-educational classes or reading books. It is a skill of focused thoughts and imagination within the mind, picturing what it may be like to be in the other person's situation. Developing this skill involves rational thinking, insight, feeling, and experiential learning which will support the client's imaginative process. A very effective technique for the experiential teaching and learning of empathy is role-playing, or the use of psychodrama. Role-playing or psychodrama utilizes all of the skill components mentioned above. Role-playing activities foster a more flexible type of thinking in the offender. The shifting of roles in role-playing develops a pattern of being able to move more easily among various frames of reference. One of the major reasons personality disorders are not more interpersonally sensitive to others is not because they don't care or lack the potential, but because they never learned how to be empathetic. The skills of emotional problem solving, self-awareness, communication, and empathy must be addressed during treatment.

Addressing Cognitive Distortions

I have spent many years working with offenders and identifying the development of their internal frames of reference from early childhood to present. The offender's frame of reference contains all the rules, beliefs, values, morals, opinions, and prejudices they utilize to approach everything in their life, their view of the world, of other people, situations, problem solving, education, employment, relationships, even the type of person they may someday marry. Their frame of reference is the result of what they were told and learned from significant others in their lives such as parents, relatives, teachers, ministers, and their friends. It is also a result of significant life experiences that may have resulted in their making an early life decision. For example, if a child at the age of six experienced a parent leaving as a result of death or divorce they would feel sad and possibly angry. A decision the child may make at that time may be something like, "I will never get close to anyone again, because they will die or leave me." An early life decision like this may result in a cognitive distortion of don't get close, or don't trust anyone. It isn't very difficult to zero in on the offender's frame of reference and cognitive distortions as it may sound. The use of interventions utilizing what, when, where and how are most effective to achieve this goal. Asking "why" questions are rarely useful. However, carefully timed questions that are intended to identify detailed information using "what," "how," "when," and "where" serve to intensify experiencing. Examples are questions such as:

"What are your beliefs about other people?"

"How old were you when you first believed that?"

"What life experiences have you had that support those beliefs?"

"What do you need to know or happen in order for those beliefs to change?"

"How will you do that?"

"When will you do that?"

"How will I and others know you have changed those beliefs?"

"How do you think your life will be different if you change those beliefs?"

These types of questions direct the offender to intensify their awareness of their problematic belief system and the resulting cognitive distortion. Interventions that are not useful and many times creates resistance include those that probe for causes of the offender's behavior:

"Why do you believe that?"

"Why don't you change that belief?"

These types of interventions are generally responded to with the word "because" followed by a lengthy rationalization or justification for the rule, belief, value, prejudice, or opinion and not resulting in change. In the following chapter, we will discuss various techniques that are utilized in the cognitive restructuring of distorted beliefs.

The most common thinking errors identified and encountered in treatment of the criminal justice client, particularly those diagnosed as having an antisocial personality disorder are: (a) blaming, used to avoid taking responsibility. It is always someone else's fault or deed, (b) grandiosity, of their ability, accomplishment, and self image, I'm special, also used to minimize or maximize the significance of a problem or issue, (c) redefining, used to fit in with what they think and believe to avoid an issue or solving a problem, (d) assuming what others think, feel or believe, which provides them with the excuse to do whatever including their criminal behavior, (e) don't trust, used to keep others at a distance and to protect their secret life of criminality,

(f) don't get close, used to avoid intimacy and not make commitments, (g) excuses, used to justify their behaviors, (h) false pride, always feeling superior to others, perceives others as being weak, (i) rigid thinking, thinking in black and white terms, there are no gray areas, (j) I deserve what I want when I want it, used to demand immediate gratification, (k) screw it, used to not deal with a problem or issue, or to think, (l) women are weak, therefore they should know their place and be subservient to men, (m) make fools of, used to set others up to fail, (n) lying, used to confuse and manipulate others, and to avoid issues, (o) taking a victim stance, used to blame others for their life problems and getting others to rescue them and feel sorry for them, (p) minimization, used to avoid taking responsibility by making something insignificant, (q) power plays, used to dominate and putting others down, (r) people and the world sucks, used to justify their behaviors and to avoid empathy.

In the following chapter, I will present several cognitive-behavioral therapy models that may be used in the cognitive restructuring of distorted thinking, and have been proven effective in assisting with the identification of the offender's risk factors.

Anger and Resentment

It is not unusual for the criminal justice client to walk in the front door angry that they have been referred for assessment or treatment against their will, and are resentful toward treatment staff because they are mistakenly perceived as being part of the court system. This initial anger and resentment can generally be resolved quite effectively by orientating the offender to the agencies and treatment staff's role. However, because of the higher occurrence of personality disorders among the criminal justice client population, the initial anger and hostility is more likely a manipulative survival tactic and a symptom of their inability to separate anger from other feelings. Criminal justice clients may come into treatment angry for a wide array of reasons, including but not limited to: (a) being court ordered to treatment, (b) inability to make a distinction between anger and other feelings, (c) using anger to create drama, (d) using anger as a deflection technique to divert attention from something, (e) to keep the therapist off-balance, or, (f) genuine feelings of anger about life issues, experiences, or being treated unfairly.

Dealing with the offender's anger and lack of feelings is essential while they are available for treatment. Most are generally experienced as being out of touch with their feelings, and as being emotionally immature.

The offender diagnosed as being CD, APD, BPD or NPD feelings are experienced as being scary, and most often eliminated from the personality and replaced by behavioral symptoms. The repression of their feelings can be accurately defined as an attempted exclusion from their awareness of impulses, thoughts, and feelings, as well as self-devaluating experiences. The repression process converts the energy that would be used to feel into behavioral energy. The offender is not conscious of this process; however, they are conscious of the early life experiences, which resulted in the repression of their feelings. Sometimes the repression is only partial which implies that the feelings that are directly related to the negative experience may still be in its original form, as only part of the negative experience was repressed.

It is necessary to therapeutically work through the offender's repression of their feelings, because emotions that are not expressed linger in the background in the form of life problems and prevents the offender from letting go of negative experiences and forming new relationships. One technique that can provide the offender the opportunity to get in touch with a full range of emotions is to design your interventions that will facilitate identifying emotions by initially limiting feelings to sad, angry, glad, or scared and everything else being an action or state of being as in the examples given below.

Therapist: How do you feel being required to be here today?

Client: I'm pissed off about it.

Therapist: That is something you do, but if you were to place being pissed off into one these four feelings—sad, angry, glad or scared—where would you put it?

Client: I would say angry.

Therapist: Good. So from now on instead of saying pissed off, you will say mad or angry. Can you describe to me how being angry feels to you?

Therapist: How do you feel about the problems you have caused your family because of your arrest and conviction?

Client: I feel pretty shi—- about it.

Therapist: Again, that is something you do, but if you place being shi—- into one the four feelings we discussed, where would it fit?

Client: I would say sad.

Therapist: Great. So instead of using that word to let me, and others, know you are sad, you will say sad instead. Right?

Client: Yes.

Therapist: Describe to me how being sad feels.

Therapist: What are you feeling about the harm you caused your victim?

Client: I feel guilty about what I did.

Therapist: That's good, but guilt is a state of being, you are guilty of the offense. However, if you placed guilt into one of these feelings, where would you place it?

Client: I would say sad.

Therapist: Very good. Describe to me how being sad feels.

Therapist: How do you feel about all these charges pending against you?

Client: I feel pretty lousy about it.

Therapist: Place lousy into one of the four feelings we discussed.

Client: Scared.

Therapist: So you are scared about what may happen to you. What do you think will happen? and what being scared about this feels like for you.

I think you get the idea. The point being is that offenders unconsciously avoid their feelings by using different words to express them, because emotions are scary for them. Although you cannot force a client to identify and express their feelings, you can invite them to explore their fear and avoidance of emotional expression and ways it inhibits their personal growth. Interventions should be designed to teach the client to recognize their feelings, and to recognize the difference between thinking, feeling, and behaving, with the goal of broadening the client's identification of feelings and initiating a pro-social thinking process to manage their feelings. Learning the relationship between thinking, feeling and behavior, and how they affect each other is essential so that the client can fully understand that just because they experience a feeling doesn't mean they have to act on it.

Social Skills Training
Many criminal justice clients that have CD, APD, BPD, NPD, or are sex offenders or substance abusers are socially incompetent. Social incompetence is a lack of social skills, which is part of the sex offender's, substance abuser's and personality disorders disposition. Their failure to learn adequate social skills in childhood has led many of them to feel lonely, rejected and isolated in their communities and creating for them a number of psychological difficulties such as anxiety, suicide attempts,

poor relationships, aggression, sexual inadequacy, alcohol abuse, substance abuse, and suicidal attempts. Their lack of social skills may have been impaired in childhood because of a number of reasons, but the most common reasons I have encountered in my clinical practice have been: (a) emotional disturbances that may have impaired their learning, (b) a failure to have been provided with social skill learning opportunities, (c) inadequate role models, and (d) one or both biological parents are alcoholic, substance abusers, or have a personality disorder themselves.

The lack of social skills denies them enjoyable communication with others and from developing appropriate relationships. Every day we are exposed to a wide variety of interpersonal situations. We must interact with colleagues, peers, cashiers, bank tellers, physicians, and even the mail carrier. Communication skills that enhance the development and maintenance of intimate relationships with our spouses, friends, and family are also important. Possessing adequate social skills makes this much easier.

The severity of the offender's social incompetence must be assessed as it varies from one offender to another based on the length and severity of their life problems. For one offender the problem may be just poor eye contact, which makes them appear as being shifty to others, with another it may be every aspect of their verbal and nonverbal behaviors. These problems are commonly observed in most or all offenders in social situations.

Some typical social skills training methods you may wish to use include:

(a) role-playing, acting out real life situations such as introducing oneself to another, asking someone out for a date, a job interview, or everyday small talk with others, (b) modeling, using the therapist as model, demonstrating appropriate behavior in different situations, (c) teaching different behaviors in detail including their importance and use in social situations, (d) homework assignments, practicing newly learned behaviors in real life situations and reporting back to the group the results, (e) carefully designed cognitive-behavioral interventions which will be discussed in greater detail in the following chapter.

Developing Social Control

People who come into contact with the criminal justice system because of their illegal acting behavior as a result of having a personality disorder, or because of their substance abuse or sexual offending demonstrate a lack of social control. More often than not, their lack of social control makes it difficult to treat them and retaining them in treatment. In order to effectively treat the criminal justice client, they must be committed to maintaining their social control during the treatment process. Treatment of alcohol abuse and substance requires that a client abstain from using any substances during the course of their treatment. Treatment of the personality disordered and the sexual offender client requires they abstain from any and all illegal acting out behaviors. It is useful to develop a social control contract with the client prior to their entering a group which provides them in writing what they will do if they feel the urge to act out. The contract should list the names and phone numbers of persons they can contact prior to any acting out. The contract should be signed by the client and therapist, with copies of the contract provided to the client's supervising agent and sentencing judge. This at least provides the client with some resources if they are committed to change to assist them in maintaining their social control. A sample social control contract is available in appendix B of this text that may be utilized as is, or modified for any special conditions, which may be required.

Learning social control is a serious clinical issue for the criminal justice client because people who have social control have learned how to manage their thoughts, feeling and behaviors in age appropriate and socially acceptable ways. Persons who lack social control who have expectations about something which has not been met, may act out aggressively. Developing social control requires that the client, while in treatment, assess their frames of reference and restructure their cognitive distortions, and learning how to manage their thoughts, emotions and behaviors. The development of social skills, self-confidence, self-esteem, and self-worth all assist in the development of social control. However, the client must be motivated to achieve these goals and in taking a crack at practicing them.

COGNITIVE-
BEHAVIORAL AND OTHER THERAPIES
FOR OFFENDERS

There are many therapies that are utilized in treating criminal offenders. Some more effective than others. Unfortunately, most therapists become trained in one therapy approach and attempt to make it fit for everyone and for every problem they are presented with. This approach just does not work with criminal justice offenders because one size does not fit all. The forensic counselor/therapist that specializes in the treatment of offenders must be eclectic in their counseling approach in order to effectively work with clients that are extremely manipulative, resistant, have different frames of reference, different life experiences, come from different cultures, and present with varying degrees of emotional, behavioral and psychiatric disorders.

In this chapter, I am going to discuss a few psycho-therapies that have proven to be effective to one degree or another in treating criminal justice clients. I am not recommending or stating that one of these therapies should be utilized, or is more effective than the other. I personally utilize a number of psychotherapy approaches with clients that are compatible to their individual personalities, problems, pathologies, and needs. I am encouraging you, however, to become aware of and familiar with more than just one approach to treating criminal justice clients.

Cognitive-Behavioral Therapy

Cognitive-Behavioral Therapy (CBT) in the treatment of personality disorders, sexual offenders, general criminal offenders, and substance abusers is considered "best practice." There have been numerous studies on the effects of CBT programs for criminal offenders with promising results. One well-conducted study identified CBT as a particularly effective intervention for reducing the recidivism of both juvenile and adult offenders (Pearson, Lipton, Cleland, and Yee, 2002). Similarly, (Wilson, Bouffard, and McKenzie, 2005) examined 20 studies of group oriented cognitive behavioral programs for offenders and found that CBT was very effective for reducing criminal behavior.

What Is Cognitive-Behavioral Therapy?

Cognitive-Behavioral Therapy is a psychotherapy based on modifying cognitions, assumptions, beliefs and behaviors, with the aim of influencing disturbed emotions. The general approach, developed out of behavior modification, Cognitive Therapy (CT) and Rational Emotive Behavior Therapy (REBT), is widely used to treat various kinds of neurosis and psychopathologies, including mood disorders and anxiety disorders. The particular therapeutic techniques vary according to the client or issue, but commonly include keeping a journal of significant events and associated feelings, thoughts and behaviors; questioning and testing cognitions, assumptions, evaluations and beliefs that might be unhelpful and unrealistic; gradually facing activities which may have been avoided; and trying out new ways of behaving and reacting. Relaxation and distraction techniques are also commonly included. CBT is widely accepted as an evidence and empiricism-based, cost effective psychotherapy for many disorders and psychological problems. It is used in individual and group therapy. Cognitive-Behavioral Therapy is a generic term for different types of therapies. During the late 1950s, Arnold Lazurus thought up the term "behavior therapy." Eventually (Lazurus, 1959) expanded on the CBT model of psychotherapy to include physical sensations, visual images, interpersonal relationships, and biological issues. Arnold Lazurus' form of psychotherapy is referred to as Multimodal Therapy (MT) and is the most complete form of CBT in addition to REBT. CBT first surfaced in the 1950s as Rational Emotive Therapy (RET) developed by Albert Ellis, which was eventually changed to Rational Emotive Behavioral Therapy (REBT), which was a retort against psychoanalytic therapies. Shortly thereafter, during the early 1960s Aaron Beck developed Cognitive Therapy, which was often being compared with behavior therapy at the time to determine which therapy was the most effective. Today, cognitive and behavioral therapy techniques are combined into CBT. Cognitive Behavioral Therapy today is the main psychological treatment researched and studied.

How Is REBT Used with Criminal Justice Offenders?

Today, REBT is effectively utilized to address the criminal justice client's criminality, criminal thinking, cognitive distortions, cognitive restructuring, overcoming destructive beliefs, feelings, and behaviors (Ellis, Albert, 1977). Some common techniques that may be utilized in treating offenders includes, but is not limited to: (a) cognitive restructuring, (b) social skills training, (c) anger management, (d) conflict resolution, (e) self monitoring, (f) challenging thinking errors, (g) challenging the offender's frame of reference; rules, values, beliefs, opinions, prejudices, (h) assertiveness skills training, (i) communication skills training, (j) relaxation training, (k) homework assignments, (1) thought stopping, (m) reframing, (n) cognitive rehearsal, and (o) homework assignments.

REBT as it applies to criminal offenders proposes that irrational ways of thinking (distorted thinking) are the underlying cause of most of the offender's psychological and behavioral problems, and that offenders can recover by becoming aware of and confronting their distorted thinking and beliefs, correcting them, and developing new thoughts and beliefs. REBT focuses on *disputing the offender's irrational beliefs,* or confronting and challenging the offender's thoughts about an *event* or situation. The basic assumption here is that the offender created and continues to contribute to their problems, as well as their behavioral symptoms, by the way they interpret events or situations. One of the assumptions of REBT is based on the assumption that a reorganization of the offender's thoughts and beliefs learned in childhood, or negative life experience, will result in a corresponding reorganization of their behavior (Deisler, 2000).

The therapist's role in this process is showing the offender they have incorporated these irrational thoughts and beliefs into their frames of reference, and teaching them how to restructure their irrational distorted thoughts and beliefs, by encouraging the offender into activities that counter their distorted thinking and beliefs.

The Rational Emotive Behavioral Therapy ABC Model

The ABC model is the foundation of REBT therapy. A stands for *activating event,* which could be external or internal to the offender. B stands for the client's *beliefs, which* are distorted cognitions or their frame of reference of the world that is rigid. These rigid beliefs are irrational beliefs and take the form of rules requiring shoulds, musts, have to, and got to. When offenders hold fast to such rigid rules and beliefs, they will also be inclined to portray irrational conclusions on the basis of them. Some of these irrational conclusions present themselves in the following forms: (a) awfulizing, expressing the belief that an event or situation is much worse than it should, (b) I can't take it, saying that they cannot foresee being able to endure a situation, (c) damnation, in the form of being critical of themselves, others, or situations, (d) always and never thinking, insisting on absolutes.

C in the ABC framework is the emotional and behavioral outcome or consequences of their belief about A. The C's that are a consequence from an offender's distorted thinking about a negative A will be irrational or an inappropriate negative consequence. The consequence involves the offender's emotions that are directly associated with A, the activating event. Inappropriate negative emotions are inappropriate for anyone for one or more of the following reasons: (a) they led to the experience of a great deal of psychological discomfort and pain, (b) they motivate the offender to engage in self-defeating behaviors, (c) they deter the offender from following through with behaviors required to achieve their goals.

Dryden and DiGiuseppe 1990, state that REBT theorizes that people have the power to change their irrational thinking particularly if we assimilate three major insights: (1) past or present activating events (A's) do not cause disturbed emotional and behavioral consequences. That our belief systems about these activating events (A's) largely create our disturbed feelings and behaviors, (2) regardless of how we may have upset or harmed ourselves in the past, we now upset ourselves primarily because we continue to brainwash ourselves with our irrational beliefs, and (3) because we are human and very easily tend to upset ourselves and because we find it easy to cling to our self defeating thoughts, feelings and behaviors, we canovercome our disturbances in the long run mainly by working hard and repeatedly to dispute our irrational beliefs and the effects of these beliefs.

Rational Emotive Behavioral Therapy with Offenders

In this section, I modified the REBT treatment sequence to apply specifically to criminal justice offenders as follows:

Step 1. Focus on problems and objectives that have been clearly defined in the Problem Oriented Treatment Plan.

Step 2. Clearly define the objective being worked on in the session.

Step 3. Assess C, the emotional and behavioral consequence.

Step 4. Assess A, the activating event.

Step 5. Clearly define and assess any residual emotional problems.

Step 6. Teach the client the B-C connection.

Step 7. Assess B, the beliefs.

Step 8. Connect the irrational belief (B) and the emotional and behavioral consequence (C).

Step 9. Confront and dispute the irrational belief.

Step 10. Prepare and assist the client to accept a rational belief.

Step 11. Work with the client to gain self-confidence to practice the new rational belief through homework assignments.

Step 12. Be certain to monitor and check the client's homework assignments and modify as may be needed.

Step 13. Assist the client in working through the process.

Step 14. Provide positive reinforcement through encouragement.

When assessing C the offender's emotional and behavioral consequences connected to A the activating event, focus on both the negative emotional and behavioral consequence connected to A. For example, if the offender wishes to change a behavior that keeps them in the criminal justice system, encourage them to identify the negative thoughts and beliefs B and emotions C connected to A that they experienced being arrested as a result of A. Assist the client at this point to assess the consequences of their negative beliefs B and emotions C connected to A the activating event and the resulting negative behavior. This process utilizing the ABC model works as in figure 1 below:

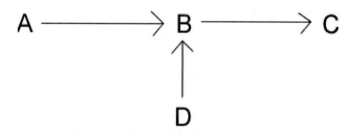

**Dispute Distorted
Thought and Belief**

The goal of the intervention should be that the client may have no control in changing external events occurring in A; however, they can create a more realistic and workable philosophy and belief B pertaining to A which will not result in negative emotional and behavioral consequences C for them. Many times offenders with personality disorders are not motivated to change. This lack of motivation is the result of their repressed emotions; therefore, they do not recognize the negative nature of the emotion they are experiencing. I therefore recommend that you assess the offender's understanding of their emotions and the self-destructing nature of their repression, which is being reinforced by their character pathology.

Some REBT therapists choose to assess C prior to assessing A; however, because of the nature of most criminal justice client's problematic behaviors, I prefer to assess A the activating event first which most times is found to be the risk factor resulting in the offender's criminal acting out behavior. However, this is a clinical judgment that is dependent upon the therapist, and the offender's presenting problem.

Assessing A, the Activating Event

Assessing A should be offense specific in order to identify the offender's risk factors, which A generally is. Be as specific as you possibly can when probing to identify the risk factor. For example, ask how often they are exposed to the activating event, how often does exposure result in their criminal behaviors, what are their thoughts about A, and what are their beliefs about A. Assist the client during the assessment of A in identifying if only part, or all of the risk factor contributing to their thoughts and beliefs about A. Because so many criminal justice clients are so adamant about wanting to sabotage their treatment, they will sometimes attempt to complicate the assessment of the activating event through the use of inferences that may or may not be real. When the client utilizes a lot of inferences, one way you may check out what is real, is by manipulating A and checking out the client's response. For example, "let's imagine that this risk factor was not present, would that have prevented you from committing your offense." If the client responds yes, it is likely that you assessed the identification of the risk factor correctly. If they respond no, then it should be clear that the probability of the identified risk factor at A is probably not real, or possibly, it is not the most important risk factor contributing to their acting out behavior. Assuming that the assessment accurately identified the client's risk factor, it is important to encourage the client to see that his thoughts and beliefs about A are a clear distortion of reality, resulting in the negative emotional and behavioral consequence in C. This process will assist in identifying the offender's cognitive distortions and beliefs that may be contributing to other identified problems.

Assessing B, the Offender's Irrational Thoughts, and Beliefs

When assessing the offender's irrational thinking and belief system use open ended questions beginning with "what" and "how." For example, "What were your thoughts about the activating event A to make you disturbed at C?" What are your beliefs about A to make you disturbed at C?" Let's assume you have a client that was arrested and convicted of child molestation. Asking them, "What were you thinking when you saw that little 6 year old girl that made you touch her?" This may identify an irrational thought and belief, and a response like "She was flirting with me, and wanted me to touch her." In this particular instance you would want to dispute the offender's irrational thought "she was flirting" and their irrational belief "she wanted me to touch her." The idea of asking open-ended questions is that they keep the offender structured, and they assist the client in identifying their irrational thoughts and beliefs about the activating event A, coming upon a vulnerable child. It also assists in identifying other risk factors that may require some special conditions related to treatment and the offender's supervision in the community. For example, avoiding places where small children would be such as schools, playgrounds, fast food restaurants, etc.

Making the Connection between A, B, and C

Before proceeding to dispute the offender's distorted thinking and irrational belief, be certain that the offender fully understands the connection between A the activating event, and B their distorted thought and irrational belief, and the negative emotions and behavior consequences at C. Using the example above, you might ask the offender if they understand that, "As long as you think that little children are flirting with you, and you believe they want you to touch them, you will continue to be fearful about being caught and incarcerated." If they respond yes, you can now begin to bring forth the A-B-C connection, for example, "So, in order to change your being fearful of being arrested and incarcerated for the same thing again, what do you think you will need to change?" If the client responds that they understand that they had better change their thoughts and beliefs about small children in order to stop being fearful of arrest and incarceration, this indicates that they understand the ABC concept. In the event they do not understand the connection between A, B, C, continue to assist them to understand the connection before you begin to dispute their cognitive distortions and irrational beliefs.

Disputing Distorted Thinking and Irrational Beliefs

The primary goal of disputing in REBT is to assist and encourage the offender to grasp and fully understand that their distorted thinking and resulting irrational beliefs are counter-productive and prevents them from living a pro-social lifestyle because they are not consistent with reality and social values.

During the disputing process ask questions seeking evidence of their distorted thinking and irrational beliefs such as, "What evidence do you have that supports your distorted thinking that little girls are flirting with you?" What evidence do you have that supports your irrational belief that little girls want to be touched?" Be unrelenting in your responses, disputing their distorted thinking, and irrational beliefs until you get across to the offender that there is no evidence to support their distorted thinking or irrational beliefs. Use a variety of disputing strategies such as: (1) focus on the irrationality of the distorted thinking and irrational belief, assisting the client to understand, (2) focus on empiricism, that their distorted thinking and irrational beliefs are based on their practice of them, not scientific evidence, and (3) focus on pragmatism, to show the offender that by continuing their distorted thinking, and holding on to their irrational beliefs, nothing will change for them.

If you are successful in disputing the offender's distorted thinking and irrational beliefs associated with the thought, assist the offender with replacing them with a new rational thought and belief about A the activating event. Once this is achieved, the next step is encouraging the offender to practice the new thought and belief through homework assignments that are directed at the offender assimilating and strengthening their conviction in their new rational thought and belief.

Cognitive-Behavioral Social Skills Training

Cognitive-Behavioral Interventions (CBI) can be a very practical and effective approach for therapists to remediate social behavioral deficits and excesses by providing the offender with the tools to control their own behavior.

Cognitive-Behavioral Interventions incorporates behavior therapy, which includes modeling, feedback, reinforcement, and cognitive mediation, which includes self-talk, and thinking-aloud to build a "coping pattern." For example, avoiding a verbal or physical fight when provoked can be mediated by inner speech such as "That really angers me, but first I need to calm down and think about this and any possible consequences." The basic assumption of a cognitive-behavioral intervention is that overt behavior such as a shy individual meeting someone, asking someone out for a date, attending a social event, attending a job interview, can be mediated by cognitive events such as "I will ask him/her out for a date, I really like him/her." Cognitive strategies incorporate a "how-to-think" structure for clients to use when modifying their behavior rather than any unambiguous "what to think" instruction from their therapist. Most importantly, the cognitive-behavioral interventions are a client function, thereby allowing the client to generalize their newly learned behavior much more than would a therapist function that will generally rely on a positive or negative reinforcement procedure.

Reality Therapy and What Is It?

Reality Therapy (RT) was developed by (William Glasser, 1965) during the middle 1960's. RT has a few things in common with REBT in that it moves the client away from dwelling on the past and focuses on the client's here and now self-defeating behaviors. It also shares with REBT in that it is a directive approach and is also didactic and action oriented. However, unlike REBT, it recognizes the problems that are inherent in labeling antisocial behaviors "irrational" and instead uses the term "irresponsible." Reality therapy, however, does not hesitate to point out any identified irrational thinking the offender may participate in, just as REBT does not hesitate to point out irresponsible behaviors.

Dr. Glasser believes that those who engage in criminal activities suffer from the inability to fulfill their basic life needs adequately. If these basic life needs are not met according to RT theory, the offender will fail to perceive correctly the reality of their world, and will act irresponsibly and not recognize the consequences of their behaviors. In other words, for the offender to act responsibly, they must be encouraged to face reality, but in order to face reality, they must be assisted in fulfilling their basic life needs. The basic needs according to RT theory are the need to love and be loved, and the need to feel we are worthwhile to others and ourselves. Glasser contends that these two needs are interrelated even though they are separate, because the person who loves and is loved generally feels that they are worthwhile, and one who feels worthwhile is generally someone who is loved and can give love in return (Glasser, W, 1965). When the offender has these needs met they develop a "pro-social identity" and if they don't they develop an "antisocial identity" which results in the lack of a pro-social lifestyle and irresponsible social behaviors. They become involved with others with "antisocial identities" that justify their lifestyle and behavior be developing a set of beliefs that are oppositional to conventional community values.

Reality Therapy refers to the causes of antisocial behaviors, but also stresses that the cause of antisocial behaviors is not an excuse for the behavior. Reality Therapy is compatible with the REBT perspectives in that the offender is ultimately responsible for their own identity and resulting behaviors. Reality Therapy also asserts that there is a "growth force" within the offender that strives for a "success identity" which RT works to activate by encouraging the offender to learn who they are, how to interact with others, and how they can be accepted by others.

The RT therapist checks out with the client, whether they are getting their needs met with three basic questions that are:

1. What do you want?

2. What are doing to get what you want?

3. Is it working for you?

Glasser itemizes seven steps that the RT therapist must take to cause a meaningful change in any client's behavior, which I paraphrased and modified to specifically fit the criminal justice client).

1. Be involved with the client, develop a warm rapport, and respect the client (maintain professional decorum at all times and act as a positive role model).

2. Understand your client's personal history, but do not stress or give importance to it (review all official records, previous treatment results, arrest record, victim statements, previous correctional records, pre-sentence investigation report, police reports, etc).

3. Assist the client to evaluate their attitudes and behaviors, and assist them to discover how they are contributing to their failure identity (antisocial identity).

4. Explore with the client alternative behaviors that will be more beneficial in developing a success identity (pro-social identity).

5. After a decision has been made regarding alternative behaviors (pro-social behaviors), get a detailed commitment in writing to a plan of change (the client, probation/parole agent and sentencing judge get a copy as well as a copy in the medical file).

6. Once the commitment has been made, make it clear that excuses for not following the plan will not be tolerated. Stress that it is the client's

responsibility to carry out the plan (monitor the plan closely for compliance and confront even minor deviations from the plan).

7. Do not be punitive with the client, but allow them to suffer the natural consequences of their behavior (in the case of a criminal justice client, this could be being terminated from treatment, or being referred back to court or probation for treatment non-compliance). Attempting to protect the client from any natural consequence only reinforces their irresponsibility and denies the self-directedness of their behavior (and also "makes a fool" of the therapist).

Transactional Analysis

Transactional Analysis (TA) is a cognitive-affective-behavioral approach to psychotherapy developed by a psychiatrist Eric Berne, MD, during the middle 1950s who is well known for his books (*Games People Play*, 1964), and (*What Do You Say After You Say Hello?*, 1975). TA is an integrative approach to the theory of psychology and psychotherapy. Integrative because it has the essentials of Psychoanalytic, Humanist and Cognitive approaches. According to TA theory, a transaction is simply what happens between two or more people when they interact. Analysis refers to the exploration and explaining transactions. TA shares with psychoanalysis the assumption that human behavior is influenced by the events of early childhood.

Berne believed that the greatest strength of TA is in its use of simple and direct terms that can be easily understood by everyone. Berne, in his book (*Principles of Group Treatment*, 1966), stated:

> "Transactional Analysis because of its clear cut statements rooted in easily accessible material, because of its operational nature, and because of its specialized vocabulary (consisting of only five words: Parent, Adult, Child, Game, and Script), offers an easily learned framework for clarification."

The Parent ego state can be controlling, critical, moralizing and contains the rules, beliefs, values, morals, opinions, and prejudices just like Freud's superego in psychoanalysis theory. The Parent ego state also has a positive part to it which is referred to as being the Nurturing Parent who is not overbearing, and reacts to others in a, respectful and caring way. The Critical Parent is domineering and fault finding. When assessing the criminal justice client's distorted thinking you will no doubt encounter their frame of reference, which originates within the Parent ego state.

The Adult ego state is the executive of the personality, and is rational and logical, and objective. The Adult ego state is responsible for testing the reality of situations and mediating between the Parent ego state and the Child ego state. Again, very similar to the concept of the ego in psychoanalysis. Most times, you will not detect the Adult ego state in many criminal justice clients, which becomes a target in their treatment.

The Child ego state is the most archaic part of one's personality structure. The Child is irresponsible, spontaneous, and fun loving. Many of your criminal justice clients function almost exclusively out of their Child ego state, which is referred to as the constant Child who refuses to grow up and behave responsibly. This is a problem because for one reason or another, which will be discussed shortly, the Parent ego state (conscience) is not having any effect, and the Adult ego state is not able to test reality or to mediate.

Although the Parent, Adult, and Child sound very similar to Freud's Super Ego, Ego, and id, Berne denies they are. According to Berne the Parent, Adult and Child are only aspects of the Super Ego, Ego and id which are "theoretical constructs" that are not amenable to observation, the Parent, Adult and Child ego states are "phenomenological realities" amenable to direct observation through the process of "structural Analysis."

TA was a radical departure from Freudian theory, and during the 1970s, primarily because of its non-technical and non-threatening terms and its model of the human psyche, its terms and concepts became popular among therapists utilizing eclectic approaches as part of their individual, group and marital therapy approaches to psychotherapy. TA approaches were and still are used in criminal justice and correctional settings, as well as in community based forensic programs for offenders.

The Three Ego States of a Person

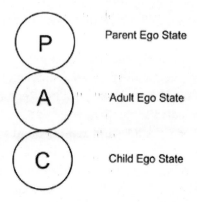

Parent Ego State

Adult Ego State

Child Ego State

Figure 2A
Healthy Personality Structure

Structural Analysis

Structural analysis is used by TA therapists working with criminal justice clients to make them aware of not only the content of their ego states, but also their functioning. The goal is that the client will become an expert in analyzing their own transactions, thoughts, feelings, and behaviors that will assist them in understanding their options to change.

The TA model of psychotherapy contends that people experience and manifest their personality through a mixture of behaviors, thoughts and feelings because they are at any given time in one of their ego states as follows:

Parent ego state (exteropsychic): a state in which people think, feel, and behave in response to their frame of reference (rules, values, beliefs, morals, opinions, and prejudices) they learned in childhood. For example, an offender convicted of domestic battery may have learned from a significant model in childhood, the "belief" that women should be subservient, and the "rule," you must put them in their place.

Adult ego state (neopsychic): a state in which people think, feel, and behave in a here and now rational and logical manner. The Adult is referred to as the executive of the personality and strengthening the Adult is the goal in treating criminal justice clients.

Child ego state: (archaeopsychic): a state in which people revert to thinking, feeling, and behaving as they did in childhood. For example, a person who doesn't get their way in a particular situation may respond by pouting, arguing, or throwing a temper tantrum. This is a commonly observed occurrence among many criminal justice clients.

Within each of the three ego states there are subdivisions. For example, the Parent ego state can be either nurturing or critical exactly like the clients biological parents were. Childhood behaviors can be either natural or adapted to others. These subdivisions describe the client's patterns of thinking, feeling, and behaving, all of which can be functional (positive) or dysfunctional (negative).

All three egos state should be separate with clear-cut boundaries as in figure 2a above. There are basically two types of pathologies that can be observed in the criminal justice client's personality structure, which is exclusion and contamination.

Exclusion occurs when ego boundaries are so rigid that the free movement of (cathexis) psychic energy does not occur. For example, a criminal justice client convicted of child molestation who views young children for sexual enjoyment exclusively, would be excluding from their personality the Parent and Adult Ego states, and be in their Constant Child ego state living their life without rules, beliefs, values, morals or reality testing as shown in figure 2b below.

The Three Ego States of a Person

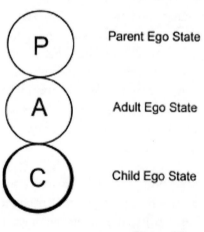

Parent Ego State

Adult Ego State

Child Ego State

Figure 2B
Constant Child

Contamination occurs when one ego state leaks into another ego state confusing the ego state contents. Contamination can occur by either the Parent ego state pushing into the boundaries of the Adult ego state, or the Child ego state pushing into the boundaries of the

Adult ego state. It is also possible for the Child ego state to be contaminating the Adult ego state, and the Parent ego state being excluded simultaneously. This particular ego state pathology is common among offenders with antisocial personality disorder and sexual offenders. When this occurs, the function of the Adult ego state becomes contaminated in its ability to be a rational, logical reality tester, and the Parent ego state is unavailable to invoke rules, values, or beliefs that may prevent the offender from acting out as demonstrated in figure 2c. For example, using the same example as above, the Adult would not be capable of making a rational decision not to molest the child, because it would be contaminated (confused) by the wants and perceived needs of the Child ego state. The process for decontaminating the ego states is cognitive restructuring, the same process as used in the REBT A-B-C model.

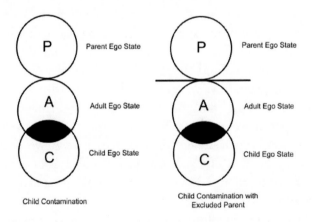

Figure 2C

Script Analysis

Scripts are "memory tapes" from childhood and other life experiences contained in our psyche. Our life script is similar to the scripts actors use to act out a part in a play or movie. As Shakespeare once said in, *As You Like It*, "All the world's a stage, and all the men and women merely players, they have their exits and their entrances" was a very accurate observation. Our life scripts determine the part we will play in the world, and will determine our exit from the world.

The most important tapes or scripts were recorded in our psyche in early childhood, because children accept messages from parents, relatives, teachers, clergy and other authoritative figures unquestionably. The messages communicated during this critical period of child development contribute to our future evaluations of ourselves as being okay or not okay people. As we mature and become old enough to question these early life messages regarding our okay-ness, it is strongly influenced by the scripting we were exposed to during our early developmental years. If the messages we received is that we were loved, nurtured, and respected, we will perceive ourselves as being okay. If we were physically, emotionally, or sexually abused and did not receive love and nurturing, we will perceive ourselves as being not okay and not develop into psychologically healthy human beings. As you have already figured out and observed, many of your criminal justice clients do not perceive themselves as being okay and have experienced physical, emotional, or sexual abuse, many in addition to abuse were also deprived of love and nurturing. Their life position based on their life scripts have become I'm not okay and you're not okay.

The criminal justice client's life script is well matched to their frame of reference and is reinforced by the client "redefining" or distorting reality in order to match their preferred way of seeing the world. For example, if a client's "belief" is that people cannot be trusted, and someone is kind to them, they may redefine kindness as the person is trying to con them out of something. Another way clients typically reinforce their frame of reference and maintain their life scripts is through "discounting" by taking something as being worthless. For example, a therapist who may be providing factual information disputing an irrational thought, the client may choose not to see the therapist's point, or may over-adapt to the therapist by telling them what they want to hear, but not believing it. As a result, many walking through the front door of your counseling center are living out their life scripts, and are not psychologically healthy human beings. The process for re-writing the life script is cognitive restructuring of their distorted thinking, which may result in positive feelings and a prosocial lifestyle.

Game Analysis

According to TA theory, a game is a series of transactions that is complimentary, or ulterior, which results in a predictable outcome. Games can be played by any one of the ego states, and generally have a fixed number of players. Games are considered to be unhealthy because they have hidden agendas.

Games are very much a part of counseling criminal justice clients. Offenders are very good at playing games, they've had a lot of practice, and often really good therapists get caught up in their games without realizing it until they are left with an uncomfortable feeling. Therapists need to be able to quickly learn to identify the offender's games and expose them immediately, because they are dishonest and work to maintain the offender's negative life script and distorted thinking. The most common games you will encounter working with criminal justice clients are: "Poor me ain't it awful," is usually played to get the therapist to feel sorry and sympathetic toward them in hopes the therapist won't make to many demands upon them. "How do I get out of here"?, is usually played by jail wise or treatment wise offenders that have learned to "over adapt" to whatever the therapist says by telling them what they think they want to hear. They may even go as far as visiting a local library to study the therapy approach the therapist is utilizing, so they can use the appropriate therapeutic language to explain their behaviors in order to appear they are gaining insight into their reasons for offending which is something every good therapist wants to hear. An excellent example of this game occurred with one of my court-referred clients a few years ago. After his third session, he approached me asking, "At what point in treatment will I be working on his wounded inner child."

It took me a minute to get myself together before I responded back to him "Well, at this point in your treatment, your wounded inner child is a deeply disturbed juvenile delinquent suffering from a severe case of diarrhea that is making a mess for everyone, and as soon as he takes an Imodium to stop the diarrhea, I'll feel more comfortable working with him. How does that sound?"

I felt it necessary to explain to him that the diarrhea

was his acting out behaviors, and as soon as he chose to maintain his social control and not act out, then we would explore his inner child. This was a combination of "How do I get out of here," and "poor me." "If it wasn't for" is a game played by offenders to avoid responsibility and being accountable by always blaming someone else or thing for either their behavior or situation. "Gee your great doc" is a game to con the therapist by telling them, "What a great job your doing, doc. I can't believe how my thinking, feeling and behavior is changing," while they continue to behave irresponsibly. "Look how hard I tried" is a game that you will encounter from those offenders that have failed in treatment several times in an attempt to sabotage their present treatment and continue their life scripts. "I tried so hard, but nothing seems to work." There are at least a dozen or more games that criminal justice clients as well as other clients use to avoid getting well. It is strongly recommended that those therapists that are interested in TA and game analysis read "Games People Play" for an in-depth understanding of game dynamics.

Transactional Analysis Proper

TA is not just a theory of personality and systematic psychotherapy, it is a theory of communication that assists in analyzing transactions between and among individuals, which can be either "complimentary," "crossed," or "ulterior." The nature of the criminal justice client's transactions are important to understand in order to determine their pathological communication style as well as the problems within their interpersonal relationships.

A complimentary transaction occurs when either a

verbal or a non-verbal message referred to as the "stimulus" is sent from one ego state of the sender, which is received by and responded to the sender from the receiver from a complimentary ego state. Some examples of complimentary transactions are as follows:

Therapist: "You didn't do your homework assignment." (Parent to Child)

Client: "Stop hassling me. I'll do it tonight." (Child to Parent)

Therapist: "Did you complete your homework assignment?" (Adult to Adult)

Client: "Yes, I did." (Adult to Adult)

Therapist: "Let's have fun today and have a bragging session." (Child to Child)

Client: "That sounds great, I want to go first." (Child to Child)

A crossed transaction is considered a failure to communicate where the therapist and client are in different ego states as follows:

Therapist: "Did you complete your homework assignment?" (Adult to Adult)

Client: "Stop hassling me, I'll do it tonight." (Child to Parent)

This type of crossed transaction is likely to produce a problem for this client. The therapist may respond back with a Parent to Child response something like:

Therapist: "You have a bad attitude and I'm sending you back to court." (Parent to Child).

An ulterior transaction is complimentary but contains a social message as well as a psychological message. Many times the criminal justice client because of their distorted thinking may believe that what is being said (social message) may have another meaning (psychological message) as follows:

Woman: "I have a great collection of baseball memorabilia. Would you like to see them?" (Adult to Adult)

Male: "Yes, I'm also a collector." (Adult to Adult) (Hidden meaning because of distorted thinking: "She really wants to have sex or else she wouldn't ask me up to her place to look at memorabilia.")

This type of communication misinterpretation occurs frequently with most criminal justice clients and most sex offenders that present with distorted thinking.

Woman: "I have a great collection of baseball memorabilia. Would you like see them?" (Adult to Adult), but body language and tone of voice indicates sexual intent (Child).

Male: "Yes, I'm also a collector." (Adult to Adult), said

with a wink and grinning (Child accepts the hidden motive).

Transactions in TA are diagrammed as follows:

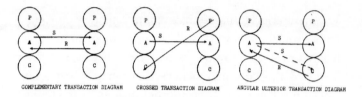

COMPLEMENTARY TRANSACTION DIAGRAM   CROSSED TRANSACTION DIAGRAM   ANGULAR ULTERIOR TRANSACTION DIAGRAM

Figure 2D
Transactions

Directive Counseling

The theories we examined above can be described as being directive therapies were all developed by traditionally trained psychiatrist's and psychologist's who were in one way or another dissatisfied with non-directive approaches utilized in traditional psychoanalysis as well as the length of time required to effectively treat clients. All of the above-examined theories were designed to identify and effectively deal with client problems swiftly and in a cost effective way. The designers of all of the examined theories we discussed above, all realized that most clients, especially the criminal justice client does not respond well to non-directive approaches, and that they must be assisted in their attempt to become responsible, rational people if they are ever to live a prosocial lifestyle.

Psychodrama and Role-play in Developing Empathy

In my clinical practice I have found psychodrama and role-play to be very useful therapeutic tools when working with clients in developing empathy, especially those client's with antisocial personality disorder and sex offenders. Psychodrama is a multimodal psychotherapy therapy developed by J.L. Moreno that integrates various features of Gestalt therapy, Existential therapy, and Transactional Analysis. Psychodrama is a therapeutic technique for criminal justice client's to express their psyche and explore representations of the past, present, and future in the here and now. (Moreno, 1972) emphasized that the primary goal of Psychodrama was to assist clients in discovering their inner truth, express repressed emotions, and create authentic relationships with others.

The basics of Psychodrama involves group members assuming various roles. The central character is the group member who presents the theme of the group drama. Supporting egos are represented by group members who assume the role of the victim in the central characters drama. Moreno labeled the audience those group members who witness the drama and represent the world at large (Jeffries, 1998). Once the drama presentation is completed group members share their individual experiences, feelings, here and now awareness, and thoughts regarding their own life (Blatner and Blatner, 1997). Additionally, I have found that psychodrama is very flexible allowing for quite a bit of creativity on part of the therapist. A therapist can easily integrate other psychotherapies such as cognitive therapy, behavior therapy, hypnotherapy, reality therapy, and TA, which all fit quite comfortably into the psychodrama group therapy model. According to (Yalom, 1975) the powerful psychodrama experience, group members gain an awareness of the universal nature of pain, death, aloneness, and individual responsibility. These struggles become a shared experience, which works to reduce associated shame and fear so often felt. (Yalom, 1975) also suggested that participation in a group allows for members to learn how to resolve conflicts and be more empathic. Yalom's research also indicates that through the sharing of information about the process of psychosocial transformation is often helpful to other group members

GROUP THERAPY

Group Psychotherapy is a treatment approach during which one or two therapists work with a small number of people within a group setting. Group therapy can take on many therapeutic forms such as "talk," "psychodrama," or "expressive" therapies such as art, music, or dance therapy. However, the contemporary treatment of general criminal justice clients, sex offenders, and substance abusers is cognitive-behavioral group therapy with co-therapists all of which is considered today to be best practice for treating the criminal justice population. The treatment of criminal justice clients with character pathologies has always, and continues to be, a source of frustration for not only the therapist, but for the offender as well. Treatment of criminal justice clients with this kind of defensive structure makes treating them a "a long hard pull" and tricky process, making the probability of transference and counter-transference reactions immense. I always stress to therapists that want to specialize in treating criminal justice clients that successful treatment of criminal justice clients with character pathologies is long term. How long treatment will take is dependent upon the "length" and "severity" of the offender's acting out behaviors, distorted thinking and beliefs, and their developmental interferences. It is reasonable to assume that there are no "short-term solutions" for "long-term problems."

One of the major obstacles to effective criminal justice counseling is the oppositional stance criminal justice clients take. Many offenders are hardcore street people that live by a street or gang code. They attend their counseling sessions only because it is not considered a violation of their code, but rather as a tactic of compliance to be released from probation, parole, a drug court, or a diversionary program. So being in counseling for these offenders is a "necessity" and not a genuine concern for self-improvement or rehabilitation. Therefore, criminal justice clients that have been mandated by the court to attend a treatment program designed to change criminal behavior and thinking patterns may spend much of their time in counseling telling other offenders how they are "getting over" on the system and the program, thereby maintaining their "street" image. However, in spite of themselves some criminal justice clients will get well if they encounter an experienced, trained, and skillful forensic counselor/therapist. Unfortunately, group therapy for criminal justice clients doesn't have a very good reputation for successful outcomes. This is in part because of poorly trained counselors and poorly designed programs that perceive all criminal justice clients as having the same problems, and therefore, all clients regardless of their needs are placed in the same group. To make matters even worse, many programs pack in 20–30 clients in one room because it is "cost effective" and viewing videos is defined as being group therapy, which in reality it is not. These types of programs not only do nothing to assist their clients in changing their criminal behavior and thinking, they reinforce the client's distorted thinking that "nothing is real" and everything is "crooked." That's unfortunate because it reflects on all the skillful and competent therapists that ethically treat their clients.

There are some techniques we will be discussing that can be used to increase the probability of developing a positive working group. The various techniques we will be exploring have been adapted and modified from the works of a number of group therapy experts in order to fit our character-disordered population.

Group Needs Assessment

The very first step in establishing a group for criminal justice clients with character pathologies is doing a group need assessment. The purpose of doing the needs assessment is to determine what the gaps are and what is needed to serve this population. You can utilize a number of methods to assess the need for specialized groups such as staff meetings, surveying the court and probation department, and parole agents. You must first determine what kind of groups are needed to serve the population effectively. For example:

1. All women's group

2. All male group

3. Substance abuse group

4. A homogenous group (e.g., substance abusers, batterers, character disorders, sex offenders)

5. Psychoeducational groups

6. Focus groups

7. Closed groups

8. What type of activities will you use if any (e.g., psychodrama, role-plays designed to develop victim empathy)

9. What will the goals be (e.g., restructure distorted cognitions to enhance a pro-social lifestyle in the community)

Once you have compiled all your information from your needs assessment, and have decided that a criminal justice client group is needed, your next step is to determine if you have the necessary and relevant skills to run a criminal justice client group, and will the group be run by a single therapist or co-therapists. This practice is laid down as one of the ethical guidelines of the Association for Specialists in Group Work (ASGW, 1998). Section B2 of the ASGW guidelines states:

Group Workers have a basic knowledge of groups and the principles of group dynamics and are able to perform the core group competencies, as described in the ASGW Professional Standards for the Training of Group Workers. In addition, group workers have adequate understanding and skill in any group specialty area chosen for practice (psychotherapy, counseling, task, psychoeducation), as described in the ASGW Training Standards.

Group Screening Process
Not all criminal justice clients are good candidates or appropriate for group therapy. You cannot simply put

a group of offenders together to see what will happen. Unfortunately, this has been an all-to-frequent practice in programs treating criminal justice clients. I can guarantee you that if you place six inappropriate clients not wanting to change their criminal behavior in a group with two appropriate clients that are motivated to change, you will very shortly have eight clients with no motivation to change their criminal behavior. There are established criteria for determining if a client is appropriate for group therapy or not which may or may not fit for the criminal justice client. According to Rutan and Stone1984, they suggest that a good group candidate should meet the following criteria:

1. The client's ability to experience and reflect upon their interactions as an indicator of ego capacity.

2. The client's ability to take on a variety of roles. For example: being a leader, and being a follower.

3. The client's capacity to acknowledge their need for others.

4. The client's ability to give and receive feedback appropriately, and

5. The client's capacity for empathy.

Friedman 1989 suggested that the ideal group candidate are those that meet the following criteria:

1. They define their problems as being interpersonal.

2. They are committed to change in their interpersonal behaviors.

3. They are willing to be influenced by the group.

4. Engage readily but not inappropriately in self-disclosure.

5. They are willing to be of help to others in the group.

At this point, you must be thinking "yeah right," when do I ever have these types of criminal justice clients referred to me? Your right, so there has to be a different screening criteria specifically for the criminal justice client. I suggest the following criteria for accepting criminal justice clients into a group, which will avoid problems for you, the client, and the group as a whole:

1. The client must admit their guilt to the present offense of which they were convicted.

2. The client must agree to attend all sessions "on time."

3. The client must state that they want to change their criminal behavior.

4. The client must commit to follow their treatment plan, and participate fully in each group session by staying focused on their treatment plan problems and objectives.

5. The client must agree that they will accept confrontation from others, confront other's behaviors when appropriate, and provide meaningful feedback.

6. The client must not be on any prescribed mind-altering psychotropics, or illegal substances that would interfere with their functioning.

7. The client must not be in need of detoxification from alcohol or other substances.

8. The client is not mentally retarded, or suffering from a neurological disorder

Meeting with the client individually for a screening interview should take about a half hour. This is time well spent as it not only allows you to determine if a client is eligible for your group, but it also allows time for you and your client to become acquainted. One of the important predictors of a positive outcome in treatment is the quality of the therapeutic alliance (Martin, 2000). Therapeutic alliance can occur during this half hour interview if the therapist and criminal justice client can agree on the goals of the proposed therapy, the tasks of therapy, as well as the conditions of therapy. You will notice that the majority of the criteria above contains a lot of "musts." If handled appropriately utilizing motivational techniques, the "musts" should not be a deterrent in developing a therapeutic relationship and will improve the probability of the client agreeing. The reason for so many musts is because of the oppositional nature of the type of client being screened. Getting such clients to initially adapt is a start in the right direction, which will strengthen the possibility of developing a working and cohesive group of clients making positive changes. Clients that indicate they will not comply can be seen individually until they are ready to comply with the group admission criteria, or they can be placed in a separate group with other clients that refuse to comply and don't meet the above criteria, with a therapist that is trained in working with heavy resistance and denial.

My clinical experience with those clients who initially refuse to comply is that approximately 33% will improve and make positive changes, and approximately 25% will drop out or be returned to the court for non-compliance. The remaining 42% will leave treatment the same way they came in with no change in attitude or behavior. You will see them again.

Advantages of Group Therapy for Offenders

Group therapy for criminal justice clients is a powerful therapeutic tool that has many advantages over individual therapy. The only two disadvantages that I am aware of are:

(a) less time for each client, and

(b) less confidentiality because of the group setting.

However, the advantages far out weigh these two disadvantages as follows:

1. Offenders learn needed skills faster by observing and reflecting on their own and other group members' social skills.

2. Client's receives feedback from their peers about concerns, issues, and life style problems.

3. Clients share similar problems and express empathy toward each other.

4. Group is a powerful dynamic environment offering an opportunity to benefit both through active participation and through observation.

5. Easier to explore issues and dynamics in a social context that more accurately reflects real life.

6. Clients learn from each other.

7. Offenders find it more difficult to lie, con and manipulate in a group.

8. Emotional and social support may be available while working through issues in a supportive, confidential environment.

9. Easier for clients to change their lifestyle behaviors through the group process.

Although there are so many positive advantages to group therapy, individual therapy should not be excluded. Criminal justice clients need to be allowed individual sessions as may be needed; however, the criteria for having an individual therapy session must be that the client has an issue that they cannot share, or they feel uncomfortable sharing in a group session. For example:

(a) a client has issues regarding their sexuality or sexual identity,

(b) a client is a witness in another criminal case,

(c) the client is being pressured by his gang members for whatever reason, and

(d) client is fearful to share all his past crimes and secret life, etc.

The therapist needs to carefully evaluate the legitimacy of the reason for having an individual session, and if granted, the client must agree that at some point when they do become comfortable with the issue, they will eventually share it in the group unless it would make the client vulnerable to being harassed, harmed or of being made a scapegoat for others. Evaluating the legitimacy of requests for individual sessions by the therapist is important, because some clients will request individual attention to "make fools" of the therapist by conning them.

Advantages and Disadvantages of Individual Therapy

Individual therapy with criminal justice clients can be a powerful and productive therapeutic tool if utilized appropriately and effectively when legitimately needed. There are many advantages to individual therapy; however, there are more disadvantages for you and the client that must carefully be assessed as follows:

Advantages
1. More confidentiality
2. More client time
3. More comfortable for the client
4. Reduces client's anxiety

Disadvantages
1. Easier to con and manipulate the therapist
2. Easier to maintain secrets
3. Client gets no peer feedback
4. Less learning experiences
5. No peer support

In addition to the above disadvantages is the clinical dilemma that individual therapy is expensive, and that most criminal justice clients, if they are employed, are in menial types of employment making minimum wage with no insurance benefits. That's a reality and a dilemma for the therapist and the client as well.

Homogeneous V. Heterogeneous Groups

Group therapy provides the criminal justice client a safe place where they have the opportunity to work out their behavioral and emotional problems. Therapy groups may be homogeneous or heterogeneous. Homogeneous groups are those whose members all share a similar diagnosis such as, substance abuse, depression, anxiety, or personality disorder. Heterogeneous groups are those whose members have a mix of diagnostic impressions, problems, and issues.

It is important for criminal justice clients to be separated and treated in groups with other group members that share similar problems, because each group must not only be "offense specific" but also share similar problems that may contribute to their criminal behavior. In the following chapter we will discuss criminal justice client groups that are offense specific, and do require homogeneity such as sex offender groups, domestic violence batterers groups, substance abuse groups, dual-diagnosis groups, and general offender groups.

Preparing the Criminal Justice Client for Group

Unfortunately, it has also been a practice of many therapists working in criminal justice settings, agencies and private forensic programs to simply assign a criminal justice client to a group without any preparation or orientation as to what group therapy is, how a group works, or even as to what expectations there are as to the client's participation in the group. This lack of preparing the client for group many times results in high drop out rates or at the very least a non-participating client "doing nothing." It is considered best practice to prepare clients for the type of group experience awaiting them. There is empirical evidence as well as expert agreement on the objectives that should be achieved by preparing the client for group (Piper and Ogrodniczuk, 2004) which fall into the following four categories:

1. To reduce the client's initial anxiety and misunderstandings about being in a group.

2. Set up favorable conditions for beginning a therapeutic alliance.

3. Achieve agreement between the client and therapist on the objectives of the therapy group.

4. To provide information and instruction to the client about group therapy to facilitate the client's ability to provide informed consent.

Most programs that specialize in treating offenders usually bypass this important group preparation process, because they are not screening their clients as to their appropriateness for group therapy to start with, and also because the attitude has been that the client is court mandated and therefore they have no choice. The criminal justice client does have choices, and should be advised of the nature of the group they will be entering as well as the group's goals. Because the groups consist of all criminal justice offenders that share some common characteristics such as being arrested, criminal thinking, cognitive distortions, and lack of social control, the treatment goals should be offender specific:

1. Take responsibility for their criminal behavior.

2. Learn to identify and understand their patterns of criminal acting out behavior.

3. Learn relapse prevention and other management skills to reduce their risk of re-offending.

4. Change their cognitive distortions and beliefs, and develop thinking skills and behaviors needed to live a pro-social lifestyle within the community.

5. Identify high-risk factors that contribute to their offending.

In addition to being oriented to the group's overall goals, the client should also be orientated as to how the group works, what is expected from them while they are in group, and how they can participate in group so they may gain the most from their group experience, at the very least:

1. They must participate by providing feedback to other group members when it is appropriate.

2. They must confront others on their self-defeating behaviors.

3. They must accept confrontation from others.

4. That it is acceptable for them to express their feelings.

5. That they must focus on their treatment plans problems and objectives.

6. That they are not expected to "monopolize" the group by going on and on to provide the other members with information about self, problems, or others.

7. They must utilize self-disclosure.

8. They must take responsibility for their criminal behavior and discuss it in group.

9. They will explore and be open to changing their cognitive distortions and beliefs.

10. They must explore and identify their high-risk factors contributing to their criminal behavior and develop a relapse prevention plan.

11. They will keep a journal in which they will write their thoughts, feelings, and reactions to problem situations to encounter and discuss them in group.

12. They will participate in homework assignments outside of group.

The next step is explaining to the client what the rules are for participating in a group. Since we are dealing with a population that doesn't like rules I suggest that you keep them to a bare minimum, for example:

1. There will be no violence or threats of violence. Violation of this rule is immediate termination and referral back to court/probation.

2. No use of alcohol or drugs while in treatment. Violation of this rule may require that you participate in a substance abuse group in addition to your regular group and an additional fee.

3. You are required to submit to random urinalysis tests when requested.

4. You are required to submit to a random polygraph when requested (generally only utilized in sex offender groups).

5.   You are required to attend every session on time.

6.   You are required to pay your treatment fees as agreed to in your financial agreement.

7.   You are required to follow all treatment recommendations and participate in all therapeutic activities.

What we just reviewed may seem to many of you as being a very directive and structured approach to preparing criminal justice clients for group therapy. Unfortunately, most criminal justice clients need a directive and structured approach in order to move them from "doing nothing" to "doing something." It is important for them to fully understand what is expected of them. If they don't know or they don't understand what is expected of them they cannot participate meaningfully in treatment.

Preparing the criminal justice client to participate in group therapy varies somewhat from other types of groups that don't work with this population; however, because of the severity of their character pathologies, it is necessary for them to fully understand what is facing them and what is expected from them. Preparing the client for group will reduce many of the inherent risks of group therapy that we come upon when working with this population, and increase the probability of developing a working group.

Confidentiality
Clients should be advised of the need for confidentiality, and that they should not discuss anything that went

on group that could possibly reveal another members identity. The client should be advised as to the significance that confidentiality must be maintained in order to maintain an atmosphere of trust, which is essential in order for group members to feel safe in disclosing their thoughts, feelings, and behaviors. The client should also be advised of the limitations of confidentiality as well as any consequences that may occur resulting from violating the confidentiality of other group members.

For the therapist, a strict adherence to confidentiality regulations builds trust. If confidentiality is broken, serious legal and personal consequences may result. Every therapist should be thoroughly familiar with both State and Federal laws on confidentiality and relevant agency policies. Confidentiality is recognized as "a central tenet of the practice of psychotherapy" (Parker, et al, 1997).

Group Developmental Stages and Process

Offender groups, like all therapeutic groups, change and evolve during the life of the group. Knowledge of group developmental stages in offender groups most times assists the forensic therapist to determine if group member behaviors emulate individual or group developmental problems. When an outpatient or residential offender group is put into practice, the therapist established limitations, which will influence the group's development. Another variable effecting offender group development is that most offender groups are open-ended groups, meaning that new members are admitted when there is an opening in the group as a result of a client being terminated or dropping out. The life of an open-ended group can go on for months or years. I personally conducted an open-ended offender group for twelve years.

There are many models and studies on group developmental stages, but even with the many variations in the name of the stages, and number of developmental stages shared common characteristics can be recognized (Wheelan et al., 2003). A review of the literature indicates that there is a strong consensus for a five-stage model of group development; however, I do not feel that they are compatible to offender groups. (Corey, 2000) discusses four stages of group development, which I have modified to apply to groups with criminal justice clients. It has been my clinical experience that these developmental stages as well as the dynamics and issues within each stage applies to homogenous groups comprised of general offenders, sexual offenders, domestic violence batterers, and substance abusers. The modified stages of group development for offender groups are as follows:

Stage 1. Trust vs. Mistrust

Most offenders have difficulties in their interpersonal relationships with others primarily because of their reluctance to trust or be intimate. During this first stage of development, group members must learn what they all dislike, "rules." They must also learn how they will participate in group, what to expect, and how the group functions. During this process the members test out the environment, the therapist, and each other as to whether this is really a safe place to discuss problems and share information about their lives. Safety is a primary issue during this initial stage. Group members will experience high levels of anxiety as they struggle in the sharing of information about their offense and self-disclosure.

All during this initial stage of group development, the offender will be constantly struggling with trusting other group members and how to participate. Eventually the group member will define their place within the group, and learn respect and how to respond. Slowly, trust and group cohesion begins to develop.

During this critical stage of group development, the therapist must develop rules and structure and be consistent in enforcing them. It is imperative that the therapist at all times model therapeutic behavior, be open, honest, and psychologically available for the group. It is not helpful or very professional for the therapist to utilize street language or profanity in group in their attempt to develop rapport with the group members. This only serves to reinforce the offenders distorted thinking and beliefs that they can "get over" on the therapist. The forensic therapist function during this stage is to also assist group members in identifying their cognitive distortions, assist in identifying and expressing their feelings, developing interpersonal skills, and make possible the attainment of group goals, assist clients in resolving conflicts, establishing group norms, and being supportive.

Stage 2. Acceptance vs. Rejection

During stage 2, member concerns about being accepted by the group or being rejected will continue to be a therapeutic issue. Because of their character pathology and street image, there will be conflicts with other group members in their attempts to gain power and control. They are uncertain as to whether the therapist and other group members really care about them, or if what they are observing is just an act. Group members will continue to test the environment in their struggle to take risks and trust others, and will constantly test the therapist to determine if they are trustworthy or not. However, as negative as all this may appear, trust and group cohesion is slowly developing, as well as the members learning how to express themselves in socially acceptable ways.

One of the big issues the therapist will be required to deal with during the group's early development is dealing with the group members' resistance. Corey, et al, (1998) states that "as group is forming, we expect participants to have reservations in revealing aspects of themselves that they generally do not freely share with strangers." What they are saying is that you should recognize resistance at this stage of development as being normal. The resistance in a group comprised of criminal justice clients, resistance should be expected and not to be avoided by the therapist. Accusing the client of being unmotivated or untreatable is counter productive and will only increase their resistance. An excellent technique for dealing with the member's resistance is sharing with the member how their resistance affects you, and asking them what they are experiencing. According to Corey, et al, (1998) such modeling encourages members to express their feelings and is an important and direct way of dealing with resistance in a group. It is imperative during this initial stage of group development to provide a positive therapeutic model by dealing openly with any and all challenges directed at you. Failure to do so will only result in your losing credibility as a competent therapist with the group.

During this stage, the therapist must also continue

assisting group members in expressing here and now reactions to what may be happening within the group. Conflict is inevitable given the population being worked with and will arise. The struggle for power and control will also continue to be a group issue. When conflict is recognized, it must be confronted, inviting the group members to deal with it openly within a safe therapeutic environment. The therapist should also respect the client's present difficulties making changes.

Stage 3. Initiative vs. Uncertainty

Finally, the level of trust and group cohesion during this intermediate stage should be high depending upon the severity of the group member's character pathologies. You should observe high levels of communication as well as members taking risks, and interacting freely. Conflict will continue; however, it is dealt with directly and efficiently by group members confronting the conflict. Most group members will have gained hope that their lives can be changed, feel supported, and begin to work on goals outside of the group. The function of the therapist at this stage is to continue modeling therapeutic behaviors, and providing reinforcement of desired group behavior. It is also important during this stage to look for common themes that may occur among group members such as patterns of relationships. The therapist should continue to assist group members recognize the causal relationship between their criminal behavior and current problems in their lives. During this working phase of the group, the therapist should also recognize that the members may feel vulnerable, because they may have not yet developed coping skills to negotiate their all their life problems. The therapist should support the members by letting them know that their feeling of vulnerability is transient. This may be the thrust that they may need to adopt new behaviors that are prosocial.

Stage 4. Client Termination Issues

As a client approaches termination, the client as well as the group will experience anxiety as well as anger. The member being terminated may experience a deep sense of loss, especially if the group was a source of personal and psychological support. Expressions of sadness are common during this stage. Group members may cope by experiencing new problems along with a suspicious effort at denial or avoidance, which will most times alternate with periods of productive work within the group. However, if termination is handled effectively by the therapist, the group generally recovers rapidly.

The therapist during the time of a group member terminating, facilitates a review and evaluation of the member's progress, and making certain there is no unfinished business that needs taking care of before being terminated. Encourage the member to plan for the future and facilitate the process of both the group and member being terminated in saying good-bye to each other.

Group Techniques

Even though you went through the screening process designed to gather appropriate group members, and even though you took great caution in all the other things you have done to put together a smooth running group, you will no doubt run into members that will be disruptive or uncooperative in one way or another. In order to prevent such members from obstructing the progress of other group members, you must identify and quickly deal with these behaviors with well-designed and timed techniques. Most often, the therapist's training and theoretical persuasion will determine their selection of techniques for various problems they may encounter in group. The type of client population that you are working with should be observed in the various techniques that you choose to utilize. For example, you cannot use the same techniques in your offender group, which is directed toward making behavioral changes that are used in a geriatric group. In other words, whatever techniques you do use must be appropriate for your criminal justice client population. In choosing your techniques, it is also important to take into consideration the group member's cultural background. For example, it is not uncommon for Hispanic clients to not want to discuss any problems within their family system. If you use a technique directed at getting the client to speak about their family, it will in all probability distance the client from their group. Therefore, before presenting a technique, be certain that it respects the client's personal and cultural background.

The following techniques are appropriate and may be used for adult general offender, sexual offender, domestic violence batterers, and substance abuse groups.

Developing Trust

As we discussed in the above section on group development, one of the big issues with criminal justice clients in a group setting is developing trust. Because of their early life developmental interferences and life experiences, most criminal justice clients mistrust everyone.

It is doubtful if utilizing any techniques prior to establishing rapport with a group of criminal justice clients would have any effect at all. In fact, it would probably result in the group being suspicious and not participating at all. You as a person as well as your therapy style are the biggest factors of the level of trust in your criminal justice groups. Being patient and paying attention to the needs of individual clients and the group's needs, being respectful and responding to clients, only utilizing self-disclosure that is relevant to what is going on, sharing openly with the group as whole what your expectations are from them, asking the group what their expectations are from you, being aware of the group's anxieties and fears, and encouraging them to share openly what they are thinking and feeling, is the best approach with establishing trust in criminal justice therapy groups.

Not trusting during the initial stage of group development can take on many forms. Some members may not trust themselves and think, *Can I trust myself to follow all these rules? Am I trusting enough to trust all these others? Do I trust myself if I get angry not to harm someone in here?*

Almost always the real fear is they just don't trust other people. It's not unusual for some members to dislike each other that contribute to their lack of trust. And last but not least, they just don't trust you. Criminal justice clients don't trust the court system, and unfortunately, they perceive you as being part of the courts and being an authority figure because they were mandated to attend your program. That's a big one to overcome; however, as I stated above, if you are patient and willing to follow through with the suggestions made, you stand a better than fair chance of establishing trust with your group.

There are many signs when there is a lack of trust in a criminal justice therapy group, which include:

1. The group is unwilling to deal with conflict or denies it even exists.

2. Members monopolize group time with long drawn out stories.

3. Members keep their thoughts and feelings to themselves, or express them in passive aggressive ways.

4. They are silent.

5. They intellectualize to hide their feelings and thoughts.

6. Deny that they have problems.

7. Ignore their treatment plans.

8. Some may hide behind "rescuing" other group members.

9. They refuse to confront others or contribute when called upon.

10. They are unwilling to take their space in group.

Physical trust building exercises seldom work with this particular population because they have a tendency to sidetrack members from talking about their mistrust, and many street type clients will just out right refuse to participate. Above I shared what works for me being the person I am combined with my therapeutic style. You can give these suggestions a try for yourself, and I am certain that they will work for you, as they did for me and many other therapists as well. Once you get the group members motivated to share their mistrust, you can then move on to using techniques that develop a sense of "togetherness."

Identifying the client's fears and anxieties can be explored as a way of developing trust. Ask probing questions such as "What is the worst thing that could happen if you trusted this group"? What do you think is the best thing that would happen"? Or you can use a group imagery exercise to explore their fears. Once the fear is identified, it can be dealt with and shared openly developing a sense of community.

Another way of dealing with the clients or groups not trusting difficulties is ask questions like, "What needs to happen here in group for you to start trusting?" or "What do you need to hear to stop mistrusting the group?," or you can do an exercise allowing one of the clients to become the therapist encouraging members to share, or another exercise where you have them pair off and share with each other what it is like being in group with each other. When they complete the exercise they can share with the group what they discovered about the other, and how it feels to be in group with them.

Dealing with Initial Reluctance and Resistance

A group member's resistance can range from sulking, silence, over-adapting to you and telling you what you want to hear, to being hostile. Most resistances takes the form of verbal responses such as "I don't know," "I guess," "Maybe," "could be," or "your the man," or some non- verbal cues such as smirking, negative head shakes, physical agitation, or a defiant gesture such as keeping their arms folded across their chest. These types of resistant behaviors need to be recognized and confronted early in order to establish trust within the group as a whole.

The very first thing you must do when you identify the client's resistance is to acknowledge their feelings by reflecting them back and providing the client with the opportunity to express them. You can also share with the client that they are on probation, which is a conditionally granted privilege that they cannot be allowed to abuse. Sharing with the client "that you fully understand their desire to get out of treatment, and that you share this desire with them" provides a mutually agreeable starting point. You then may clearly delineate the conditions under which your mutual goal can be successfully achieved. Assist the client in understanding that a negative or hostile attitude or being resistant will only slow down achieving your mutual goal of them being terminated from treatment, and released from probation. Using this approach is directly from Reality Therapy, not punishing the client, but rather letting them know they will be allowed to suffer the consequences of their negative behavior is reality.

Dealing with the Tough Guy Image

In the beginning, I stated that treating the criminal justice client would be a "long hard pull." Although you're doing everything therapeutically correct, you are going to encounter the "tough guy." This is the guy that nothing seems to work and presents an extremely high level of resistance to all your interventions by simply responding with "I don't know" to everything sarcastically with a "smirk" on their face. The tough guy hides behind their image to keep others from getting close to them or confronting their behavior. Obviously this member's resistant behavior and street image cannot be ignored, and must be dealt with in group.

You may want to utilize advanced image breaking techniques designed to break through the tough guy image and resistance. For example, after having received a sufficient number of "I don't know" or other similar responses to your interventions, you may want to try this technique. Respond to the client's "I don't know" with, "I hear that you just don't know very much," so here's what I want you to do. I would like you to put your chair in the corner and stay there until you can figure out what you do know. When you get that figured out, let the group know and then you can come back into group. Expect the client to vigorously decline your kind offer to go to the corner. At this point, you calmly present the client with the following alternatives. They can go to the corner, or they can be returned back to court, probation department, or parole agent for non-compliance at which time they can explain what they do know to them. You can expect the client at this point to comply with your request because compliance in the tough guy's frame of reference is a survival technique. Rarely will you have a client take the option of being returned back to court or their supervising probation/parole agent. It is important that when the client does comply and go to the corner, that you commend them for making the right decision, for example, "I want to commend you for making the correct choice. When you want to, you can make correct choices."

The above discussed technique serves several purposes. First, it cuts across or alters the client's tough
guy image within the group, and within himself because
tough guys just don't sit in the corner like a child. Second,
the client is complying. This approach is not "punishing"
the client, because it is placing them in the position to
make a decision, and allowing the client to be responsible for the natural consequences of their behavior if they
make the wrong decision. Again, this is an approach that
a Reality Therapist would take. However, failure to follow through with referring the client back to the referral
source will result in your loss of credibility with the other
group members, and will reinforce for the client that was
requested to go to the corner their irresponsibility and
denies the self-directedness of their behavior. If you are
not prepared to follow through with referring the client
back to their referral source, I recommend that you not
use this particular intervention.

Dealing with Angry Group Members

There is no doubt in my mind that you will encounter
at least one or more consistently angry clients in your
group. I get them all the time. Most times, the anger you
are seeing from your criminal justice client is a deflection
technique used to direct you away from treatment issues.
And then again, sometimes criminal justice clients escalate anger over fear because of their distorted thinking
that "real men" don't get scared. And sometimes the client is really angry. Anger is difficult to deal with in a
group setting because most criminal justice clients have
a tendency to escalate their anger until the therapist
backs off in fear themselves and "does nothing." A cli-

ent that is truly angry and constantly utilizes anger that cannot be resolved is a poor candidate for group therapy and another treatment modality should be considered for them in addition to group such as concurrent anger management classes. In addition, an angry or hostile client can have a devastating effect on the group environment and continued development. In any event, a client that expresses anger or hostility whether it is real or not cannot be simply dismissed. I always ask myself when I encounter such clients, *What am I discounting about this client's anger, What am I not identifying that's going on with this client?* And most times the answer is simply that I have either discounted, ignored, or did not identify the client's fear. Many times with criminal justice clients the "symptom" of anger is their fear of being either vulnerable, trusting others, being intimate, or not believing they can successfully complete the program. If this is the case, and you are able to bring the fear to the surface and deal with it openly in group, the client's anger most times diminishes.

Dealing with Challenges to the Therapist

Why do criminal justice clients challenge the therapist that is working to help them change? The answer is obvious, they were mandated by the court to attend your program, and therefore you become a representation of something they have spent many years resisting. You are perceived as being an "authority figure." You are a threat to their way of thinking, feeling, and acting, and they are not particularly anxious to change, especially for someone who is part of "the system." Their challenges toward you may be interpreted as a defense designed to protect them from the feeling of loss of autonomy. In other words, it is another form of resistance to change. Psychological reactance theory states that whenever someone's sense of autonomy is threatened by forcing him or her in any way to do something, the natural response is to resist. When challenges are made toward your authority, your therapeutic approach, your qualifications or competencies, acknowledge the client's thoughts and feelings as well as their right to have their views of you, and ask that they share them openly with the group. You can also let them know that you don't particularly mind that they have these thoughts and feelings as long as they are being responsible in group.Hassling back and forth with a client that is challenging you is counter-productive in that it would only serve as a catalyst for further challenges. Instead, remind the client that their being in group is a cooperative effort on both your parts. More often than not, taking this approach generally resolves this type of resistance and problem.

Dealing with the "Doing Nothing" Client

As you already know doing nothing in treatment can take many forms. The most common form of doing nothing that we encounter with the criminal justice client is non-participation in group activities, not completing home work assignments, not fulfilling treatment plan objectives and goals, and silence. Many criminal justice clients may argue that their non-participation in group activities does not mean that they are not learning and assimilating what is going on in group. They most times respond to this confrontation by saying, "When I can relate to something I will," "I'm just a naturally quiet person," or "I learn things better by just watching what others do." At this point the therapist should direct the client to share what they have learned "doing nothing" with the rest of the group. Another tactic would be to have all the group members one at a time tell the client what they think, and how they feel when the client is doing nothing in group. It is important to move this type of group member from "doing nothing" to "doing something." Some techniques that may be considered could be: (a) homework assignments, (b) making it a point to call upon the client each session for feedback to another client, (c) inviting the client to explore what their doing nothing really means, and (d) inquiring each session if the client got what they needed from the session, and share what they got with the rest of the group.

There are also other considerations that must be taken into account that must be carefully assessed by the therapist of why the client is "doing nothing." They include, but are not limited to the following:

1. The client may have difficulties asserting themselves.

2. The client may not think they are as smart as the rest of the group.

3. The client is fearful of how the group will respond to them.

4. The client may think there is a lack of confidentiality.

5. The client doesn't want to be a group member.

6.   The client may lack trust in the therapist and the group.

7.   The client may fear being rejected or ridiculed.

8.   The client has a "don't exist" injunction from something that was said to them in early childhood.

An example of a client with a "don't exist" junction is one of my clients that really worked hard at doing nothing. He was a big man approximately three hundred pounds or more. Every group session he just sat there unless called upon. During one session, I asked him if he had any recall of his parents during his early years, and what are some things he can remember they said to him. He sat there for a few minutes before responding, and finally said that he remembers when he was six years old that his mother used to tell him when there were visitors to the home that he had to play quietly because "little boys should be seen and not heard." My response to him was, "You must have really taken that statement seriously, because here you are today twenty-nine years old weighing at least three hundred pounds and can be easily seen and still not being heard." It took quite a few sessions to work through that early life injunction and the end result was an active group member being heard. He became so active in fact that with encouragement from the group he became motivated to lose weight and when terminated from treatment he weighed 190 pounds. He jokingly said during his good-byes to the group, that he left behind another person that used to keep him in trouble referring to the 110 pounds he lost.

Developing Empathy

Criminal justice clients whether they are general offenders, sex offenders, domestic violence batterers, or substance abusers, rarely think of the feelings and psychological problems their victims, friends, and family experience because of their criminal behavior, interpersonal insensitivity, and lack of empathy. Empathy can be simply defined as "the ability to identify with and understand another person's feelings and difficulties." One of your therapeutic functions is to assist group members in developing empathy by confronting behaviors that block the understanding of empathy.

Some of the ways to encourage the client to think about their lack of empathy is to have them compile a list of the thoughts and feelings they think their victim, friends, and family members may have experienced as a result of their criminal behavior, and share them in group. Have the group members respond if they think that the responses of the victim were justified, and why they were justified. Being criminal justice clients, it is highly likely that many of them have been victims of a crime themselves at one time or another. Have the group write out a list of the thoughts and feelings that they had about their victimizers and share them with the group. You can also have the group members explore the thoughts and feelings of their friends or family members that were victimized, and again share and discuss them in group. Exercises and discussions like these will generally reveal that even criminal justice clients value "justice" when the victim and victimizer roles are reversed. Other useful techniques for assisting clients in the development of empathy include:

1. Role-Playing.
2. Reverse Role-Playing using the empty chair technique.
3. Confrontation Tactics.
4. Personalizing the Victim.
5. Utilizing Readings and Educational Videos.
6. Acting out the victim role using Psychodrama.
7. Writing a letter to the victim, friend, or family member (not to be sent to the victim) and shared in group.
8. Guided Imagery.
9. Cognitive Restructuring.
10. Hypnosis.

Spirituality

There is no doubt that spirituality and faith offers to some people hope, nurturing, and a sense of purpose, meaning, and support to continue on. The therapist should explore with their group members the importance of spirituality, and if the group members indicate that it is important, the therapist can incorporate it into group discussions. Another way of exposing group members to spirituality is to have them attend AA, NA, or OA twelve-step meetings where the importance of spirituality is discussed.

Dealing with Transference and Countertransference

Whenever transference or countertransference occurs

between group members, or between the therapist and a group member, the therapist needs to bring all feelings associated with it to awareness and manage them appropriately. Transference and countertransference issues are not negative. It is almost inevitable in a criminal justice client group. The therapist with the assistance of supervision can use transference and countertransference to support the group process (Vannicelli, 2001).

Encouraging group communication

A group norm could quickly become "we don't have to do anything but be here" if the therapist doesn't stimulate members to be active during the initial stage of the groups development. The therapist should stimulate group communication among members and themselves. Some interventions you may want to consider using to assist members engage in dialog are:

1. Assisting a member that may be having difficulty expressing a thought or a feeling, and putting the thought or feeling into words and asking, "Did I get that right?"

2. Praise good communication between members when it does occur.

3. When a client is struggling to verbalize the therapist might ask, "I see that you are struggling. I know that it's important for me, and the group. Do you have any ideas how I or the group can help you say what you want?"

4. Building bridges between members by something like, "It sounds like you two guys have a lot in common. Would you like to share them with the group?"

Dealing with Conflict

Conflict in a criminal justice group with clients mandated to attend is almost unavoidable. But just as in any other therapy group, conflict should be construed as being healthy. When conflict does occur, the therapist should take the opportunity to learn from, as it presents an opportunity for group members to explore possible connections with each other. The therapist's group management skills are crucial as the task of conflict resolution unfolds. It may not be helpful to let the conflict go too far, as it is to shut it down before it is worked through. The therapist should also be aware that a conflict between group members could be displaced anger that one member may feel toward the therapist. If this is suspected the probability should be explored with the group member by saying something like, "Jack, I notice, you have been rather upset with me for the past week about the way handled confronting you in group last week. Do you think it is possible that some of the anger you are experiencing right now belongs to me?"

OFFENSE SPECIFIC GROUP THERAPY

Comorbidity is common among criminal justice clients referred for counseling services. For example, it would not be unusual for a sexual offender to have an antisocial personality disorder and substance abuse disorder, or for the domestic violence batterer to have a substance abuse disorder and a borderline personality disorder, or the substance abuser to have a major affective disorder and anxiety disorder. Most of the time these clients are placed in homogeneous groups that are offense specific such as a substance abuse group, batterers group, sexual offender groups, and general offender groups. This is appropriate for a number of reasons such as, offenders share the same offenses and are empathetic to the problems of other group members, members are able to share details of their offense without shame or embarrassment, because they all have committed the same type offense and group members may be a source of support for each other. Generally, in these types of groups, the focus is on the offense only, and changing the behaviors leading up to committing the offense. Rarely, if ever is comorbidity dealt with or even considered to be a cause of the client's criminal behavior, except in the case of substance abuse where there has been volumes of research supporting the correlation between substance abuse and criminal behavior.

The primary problem is that the co-occurrence of disorders make diagnosis complicated and may even go unnoticed during the client's assessment. Even if it is identified and diagnosed, treatment is difficult even when a therapist is willing to take on the challenge. However, most therapists are reluctant to treat comorbidity in the sexual offender, domestic violence batterer, substance abuser, or general offender because their training has been offense specific only with no training or understanding of how to take an integrated systematic treatment approach, which is the key to treating criminal justice clients with comorbidity and changing their behavior. Unfortunately, there is literally no research on antisocial personality disorders and comorbidity that I am aware of, and very little on sexual abusers with comorbid psychiatric disorders other than psychopathy or substance abuse. In order to recover fully, a criminal justice client with a co-occurring disorder needs treatment for all their problems. Unfortunately, most criminal justice programs deliver fragmented and ineffective treatment for the criminal justice client with co-occurring disorders. Taking an integrated treatment approach is effective and can prevent re-offending behavior, as well as reduce the severity of the client's comorbid disorder, which is in the best interest of the community and client.

Domestic Violence Batterers Group

There are presently a number of therapies for domestic violence batterers available today. However, the majority of these approaches are primarily psycho-educational models that are for the most part "time limited." For example, some programs are twenty-six weeks or less to a maximum of fifty-two weeks that do not involve a comprehensive assessment of the batterer's psychosocial functioning or assessment for comorbid psychiatric disorders. At the very best assessment was limited to self-report questionnaires and a risk assessment for re-offending. How to reduce the incidence of domestic violence battering has been extensively researched and still remains unanswered. Even research in the field assessing the effectiveness of criminal justice intervention and treatment effectiveness has not been conclusive.

However, there has been research on domestic violence batterer typologies that may provide some indication as to the criminal justice client's treatment needs. Holzworth, Munroe and Stewart (1994) identified three types of male batterers. These are the "family only batterer," the "dysphoric/borderline batterer," and the "violent/antisocial batterer."

The traits of the "family only batterer" indicate that he is less likely to have witnessed family violence, is more stable, has been married longer and is more committed to an intimate relationship, is satisfied with his relationship, has more liberal role attitudes and feels guilty about his assaultive behavior.

I would suggest that an accurate assessment of this type of offender would probably not uncover any gross psychopathologies that would have contributed to his assaultive behavior. However, assessment may uncover a generalized anxiety disorder, alcohol abuse, or alcohol intoxication in which the following treatment approach would be indicated:

1.   Psycho-educational classes as defined below.

2.   Group therapy as described below.

3.   Empathy training as described below.

4.   Family therapy and education as described below.

5.   Social skills training as described below.

6.   Anger management as described below.

7.   Relapse prevention planning as described below.

The traits of the "violent/antisocial batterer includes exposure to family violence, is less stable, has multiple intimate partners, is less attached to intimate partners, is more controlling in intimate relationships, and has definite conservative role attitudes.

I would assume that an accurate assessment of this type offender would result in a diagnosis of antisocial personality disorder and alcohol or substance abuse and possibly an explosive disorder co-occurring with his domestic violence assault. Treatment of this type offender would need to be "long-term" one to two years with a therapist that is skilled in utilizing an integrative treatment model and should include:

"Psycho-educational classes" with a focus on relationships, problem solving, psychosocial dynamics of domestic vio-

lence, and on the social, medical, and psychological consequences of substance abuse.

"Anger management" with a focus on emotional control and social control.

"Group therapy" utilizing cognitive behavioral techniques and an integrative treatment approach addressing their assaultive behavior, co-occurring disorders, personality disorder, alcohol, and substance abuse, and distorted thinking.

"Family/couples therapy" and education with a focus on resolving relationship problemsand communication.

"Empathy training" utilizing role-play, psychodrama, or other empathy developing techniques.

"Cognitive restructuring "utilizing the A-B-C model to restructure distorted thoughts and feelings.

"Social skills training" directed at improving interpersonal relationships.

"Relapse prevention planning" focusing on identifying high-risk factors that lead to domestic violence and the development of new coping skills to deal with or to avoid high-risk situations precipitating domestic violence battering.

"Support group" attendance such as AA, NA, or OA.

According to Holtzworth, et al, (1994) the dysphoric/ borderline batterer falls between the above two extremes. They concluded that treatment should focus on the type of batterer in order to be most effective. My personal review of the literature on domestic violence batterers all indicate that there is no conclusive evidence that taking a psychoeducational model approach or a cognitive behavioral approach is any more effective than the other. However, I do agree with Holowitz, et al, that there should be a focus on offender typology in treatment. This makes sense because each typology when identified will present with different symptoms, diagnosis, and prognosis requiring a different treatment approach.

Sexual Offender Groups

A basic assumption in sex offender treatment is that there is no cure for sexual assault; however, sexual offenders can learn new coping skills that if practiced will assist them in controlling their sexual urges, and not re-offend. In most sex offender groups, the group goal and focus is on the identification of the offender's offense cycle and the development of a personalized cognitive-behavioral relapse prevention plan. The offender is assisted in not only the identification of their offense cycle, but also in understanding it. The offender, while in group, is also required to identify their specific pre-offense risk factor as well as their thoughts and feelings in response to their exposure to the risk factor. The offender is then assisted in identifying and understanding the progressive and self-reinforcing nature of the pre-offense risk factor and recognizing that the offense was not a spontaneous event, but rather the product of a predictable series of thoughts, feelings, and behaviors.

Most sex offender groups utilize the A-B-C model discussed in chapter 4 to cognitively restructure the offender's distorted thoughts and beliefs. It is also considered "best practice" to utilize co-therapists and a cognitive-behavioral approach in sex offender group therapy. The primary reason for this particular approach is rooted in the belief that sex offenders can continue to experience deviant sexual urges, and possibly re-offend. It is believed that treatment can assist the offender in managing their sexual urges and is not a "cure" to sexually offending again.

Like any other offense specific type of group therapy, sexual offender therapists require training, experience, and skills on the biopsychosocial aspects of sexual offending. The purpose of sexual offender treatment groups is for the offenders to develop and carry out their own relapse prevention plan. A homogenous group of sexual offenders also creates a safe place for the offender who has sexually assaulted to (a) challenge and support each other, (b) confront members denial, (c) identify their own risk factors, (d) identify new coping skills, (e) take responsibility for their present as well as past sexual assaults, (f) recognize the impact that their sexual assault has had on their victims, (g) develop victim empathy, work on regaining the trust of their family members and others, (h) and learning to control unacceptable impulses.

There are volumes of literature that addresses the effectiveness of treatment programs for sex offenders; however, it remains a specialized treatment field and most mental health practitioners remain unaware of the effectiveness of treatment (Grossman L.S, 1985), (Marshall, Ward, et al 1991), (Marshall and Pithers, 1994), (Abel, G, et al, 1985). Even in spite of treatment effectiveness and the low recidivism rate of treated sex offenders, the criminal justice system and most mental health professionals assume, and continue to argue in support of, public opinion that sexual behaviors are nothing like other mental illnesses because sex offenders are untreatable.

Sex offenders are not a heterogeneous group; however, in 1979 Dr. Nicholas Groth developed a profile of several typologies of rapists, and in 1982 two types of pedophiles (Groth, N, 1979, 1982). It is beyond the scope of this chapter to thoroughly examine each typology in depth; however, we will review the main points of each typology and identify the most common comorbid disorders for each type.

The "Power Rapist," when sexually offending, is motivated by power and control. The offense when committed may last for hours while the offender humiliates and degrades their victim. There may or may not be violence before, during, or after the offense. The primary motivator for the power rapist is "power" and "control." This type offender has multiple issues pertaining to females and their roles. There is generally no mental disorder other than antisocial personality disorder (Zonana, 1997). Alcohol or substance abuse may also be identified with this type sex offender.

The "Anger Rapist" is motivated by anger. They are known for using more force than would be necessary to commit the offense. Generally, the offense is of short duration and violent, with the victim most times requiring medical attention. The most common comorbid disorders found are antisocial personality disorder, which may co-occur with an explosive disorder and alcohol or substance abuse disorder.

The "Sadistic/Ritualistic Rapist" is considered to be extremely dangerous. The offense when committed could last for hours, days, or weeks while the offender degrades, humiliates, and tortures their victim. They become aroused by watching their victim suffer. This type of offender has progressed from antisocial personality disorder to full-blown psychopathy, which may co-occur with other mental disorders.

The "Fixated Pedophile" is an adult who is poorly adapted to socially accepted norms. Their primary sexual attraction and interests are in prepubescent children. This type offender meets the DSM-IV diagnostic criteria of Pedophilia, Exclusive Type. This type offender may present with one or more co-occurring personality disorders, alcohol or substance abuse disorder, major affective disorder, and adjustment disorders.

The "Regressed Pedophile" is primarily attracted to his/her own age group, but is passively sexually aroused by children. In most cases, their attraction to children does not manifest itself until later in the offender's life. For the most part, the regressed pedophile lives a traditional life, and the majority of times their sexual acting out against children was the result of a psychosocial stressor such as divorce, separation, loss of employment, death of a family member or friend, etc. The most common co-morbid disorders diagnosed co-occurring with the DSM IV diagnostic criteria of Pedophilia Nonexclusive Type include alcohol or substance abuse, major affective disorder, adjustment disorders, or a personality disorder.

The treatment of sex offenders varies in length; however, the programs that show the highest success rates are those utilizing a cognitive-behavioral therapy approach in their groups. Some of the cognitive-behavioral techniques that are most commonly used include:

"*Aversion therapies*" which pair the offender's deviant

sexual fantasies with a negative result (Rice, Harris and Quinsey, 1990). The offender works closely with their therapist to identify their deviant fantasy. The fantasy is then presented verbally to the offender along with a self-administered nasty odor such as ammonia. The use of ammonia capsules are also utilized outside of treatment by the offender to control their sexual urges.

"*Covert sensitization*" also pairs the offender with their deviant sexual fantasy along withmental images of suffering consequences. The offender verbalizes their fantasyand when they begin to become aroused, they stop, and then begin to verbalize an equally detailed fantasy with highly aversive consequences such as being arrested, imprisoned, ridiculed, or harmed.

"*Imaginal desensitization*" in which offenders are trained in deep muscle relaxation techniques. This technique is thought to assist the offender in controlling their sexual urges and feelings that are associated with their deviant fantasy until they recede without acting out on them.

"*Cognitive Restructuring*" is utilized because sex offenders have developed manydistorted beliefs in order to justify their deviant sexual behaviors. It is thought that offender's, regardless of their crimes, distorted thinking relieves them of their feelings of shame or guilt connected to their criminal behavior.

"*Social skills training*" is utilized because it is believed that deficits in social skills may be involved in sexually deviant behavior. However, social skills training is also utilize with substance abusers, batterers, and general offenders as well based on the belief that skills are necessary for living a pro-social life style.

"*Victim awareness or empathy*" training is utilized with sex offenders as well as with substance abusers, batterers, and general offenders because their cognitive distortions allow them to believe that their victims were not injured by their crime, and specifically for the sex offender's belief that the victim really wanted them and enjoyed the event. Empathy training techniques may involve viewing videos of victims sharing their experiences, role-playing, as well as receiving feedback from the therapist, victims, or other offenders (Laws DR, 1999).

"*Relapse Prevention*" is not only utilized in sex offender treatment, but in treatment for all types of offenders including substance abusers, batterers, and general offenders.Relapse prevention involves identifying maintenance strategies to anticipate and resist deviant urges (Pithers W,1990) and (Laws DR, 1999). The crucial elements of relapse prevention involve the offenders identifying their "high-risk" situations, and the decisions they make that bring them closer to re-offending. They learnnew skills to deal with their high-risk situations, in order to prevent reoffending.

Substance Abuse Groups

Any group can be therapeutic because of its numerous advantages, especially in substance abuse treatment as described by (Brown and Yalom, 1977). These advantages include:

1. Groups provide needed structure for those with substance abuse problems.

2. Groups provide support and encouragement to one another outside the group.

3. Groups instill hope.

4. Groups provide an opportunity to learn new social skills.

5. Groups can encourage members to abstain from substances.

6. Groups provide feedback and confrontation.

7. Group members see others in recovery.

8. Groups reduce the substance abusers sense of isolation.

Treating substance abusers in groups certainly has many advantages, as well as risks. Any type of therapy can fail completely, or yield second-rate results if the therapist is not properly trained and does not understand the bio-psychosocial aspects of addictions.

It is seldom that a substance abuse client does not present with one or more co-occurring disorders. The most common co-morbid psychiatric disorders that are identified as co-occurring with the client's substance abuse disorder are major affective disorders, anxiety disorders, posttraumatic stress disorder, various personality disorders, and adjustment disorders. The presence of co-morbidity makes it difficult formulating a primary and secondary diagnosis. Many addiction professionals believe that the substance abuse diagnosis is always primary and the behaviors, depression, anxiety, etc, are the result of the substance abuse and will disappear if the client abstains from further abuse. This may be true in some cases; however, in the majority of cases it is not. To determine which occurred first, the substance abuse or the co-occurring disorder, it is necessary to determine which one was first observed. I do a timeline, which seems to be as good as any other technique by taking a history of the client's substance abuse from their first use to the present. I then do another time line for instance, for antisocial behaviors. If the time line indicates that the client was having behavioral problems, stealing, fighting, runaway, truancy, etc, prior to the use of their preferred substance, my primary diagnosis would be Antisocial Personality Disorder. If the substance use began prior to the behaviors, my primary diagnosis would then be a substance abuse disorder. Making this distinction is important because diagnosis determines what treatment strategies will be used, as well as the client's prognosis for recovery.

Substance abuse treatment varies in the length of time an individual is in group. The most effective substance abuse groups utilize a cognitive-behavioral approach. Some of the techniques utilized in substance abuse groups are:

"*Cognitive-behavioral therapy*" as described in chapter 5.

"*Psychoeducational*" sessions on the medical, social, and psychological consequences of addiction in various life domains.

"*Social skills*" development as described under sex offender group therapy above.

"*Anger management*" techniques such as deep breathing exercises, meditation, learning empathy and stress management skills. Generally treatment is designed to the client's personal needs.

"*Conflict resolution*" techniques designed to resolve problems with others in a non threatening manner.

"*Support group*" attendance at Alcoholics Anonymous or Narcotics Anonymous as an adjunct to group therapy.

"*Relapse Prevention*" as described above for sexual offenders.

General Offender Groups

The therapist in charge of a general offender group must be thoroughly familiar with the psychodynamics of the antisocial personality structure, and be specifically trained in working with the disorder, as well as having an eclectic therapy style. General offender groups are homogeneous and comprised of offenders that are multi-recidivists with a "primary" diagnosis of antisocial personality disorder (APD) which may co-occur with a substance abuse, anxiety, major affective, or attention deficit disorder, all of which may be easier to treat than the APD; however, treating them may improve the offenders overall health and functioning. The arrest record of a general offender may indicate they have committed any number or type of crimes such as robbery, battery, forgery, burglary, sexual assault, or grand larceny. The criteria for being placed in a general offender group as above noted is a "primary" diagnosis of antisocial personality disorder with multiple arrests and convictions. It is rare that a diagnosis of APD is clear cut. In the majority of cases, the diagnosis of APD will present with narcissistic or paranoid features making treatment even more difficult. The diagnosis of APD practically contraindicates any modality of psychotherapy. The prognosis for psychotherapy is also discouraging. For example, offenders with APD that also have narcissistic features, interpersonal difficulties, rigid denial systems, a lack of impulse and social control with relentless acting out of self-destructive behaviors that are not controllable, psychotherapy is contraindicated.

Many criminal justice clients diagnosed with primary APD can be successfully treated. However, the successful treatment of APD first requires that the therapist have an agreement with the sentencing judge that treatment shall be long term anywhere from one to three years, and that if the client fails to comply with treatment, they will experience the natural consequences of their behavior and serve their jail or prison sentence. If this agreement cannot be reached, the offender will drop out of treatment or be uncooperative with no consequence. When this occurs, the program and therapist lose credibility with clients already in treatment and those that will be referred. The primary objective of long-term treatment for APD is the modification of personality features of the APD that work against their potential, and ability to engage in and maintain a pro-social lifestyle within the community.

The treatment modality of choice is group cognitive-behavioral psychotherapy. Cognitive-behavioral therapy utilizing the A-B-C model discussed in previous chapters has proven most effective in the cognitive restructuring of the APD's distorted thoughts and beliefs. Expect this process to be a "long hard pull" along with many disappointments. I have been treating this population for almost thirty years and have developed techniques that work well for me and the client; however, there is going to be a significant number of clients that you will see again after you terminate them, and they are re-arrested a short time after. The trick in not burning yourself out, or thinking your not a good therapist is to realize that the client was just not ready enough to change. Possibly, the next time you see them they have suffered enough, and are ready to take treatment seriously.

Treating the APD offender requires a different approach than the other groups we discussed above. The only purpose of this group is to address the client's APD structure and criminogenic needs. The primary techniques are:

"Confrontation" utilizing motivational techniques. If the use of motivational techniquesfails to work, then change up and use heavy confrontation. Once the client beginsto adapt (and that is a beginning) switch back to motivational techniques.

"Cognitive restructuring" techniques, preferably the A-B-C model, previously discussedso the offender can gain a good understanding of how the identified thought andbelief may be distorted.

"Transactional Analysis" techniques, especially Life Script Analysis and Ego State Analysis (Parent, Adult, Child). Game Analysis can also be used to demonstrate how their distorted thoughts and beliefs result in unproductive activities.

"Reality Therapy" approaches, when appropriate allow the offender to suffer the natural consequences of their behaviors and attitude.

"Home work assignments" to get theoffender to practice new behaviors outside of group.

"Empathy training" as explained above.

"Identifying their risk factors" to offending and developing new coping skills.

"Relapse Prevention Planning" as previously discussed above.

"Support Group" attendance at NA, AA, or OA.

"Other Treatment Modalities" as may be indicated to treat co-occurring substance abuseor other disorders.

Therapist Training and Supervision

It would be a burdensome task for a mental health professional to possess all the skills required to treat every specialty within the forensic counseling field. However, the mental health professional that chooses to specialize in one particular forensic specialty such as sex offender treatment, substance abuse treatment, domestic violence, or general offending, should have adequate training and supervision within their forensic specialty.

Mental health professionals come to the field of forensic counseling from within a wide range of educational and professional backgrounds. Some are clinical social workers, psychologists, addiction counselors, family therapists, mental health counselors, and clergy. Most of them have not had any specific training or supervision in the specialized skills needed to be effective within their forensic specialty.

Training and education within the forensic specialties for forensic counselors is critical because the traditional separate fields of mental health and criminal justice are rapidly beginning to overlap because many crimes that come to the attention of law enforcement are both a mental health and criminal justice issue. This problem has been requiring cross training and cross knowledge between the two professions.

As the forensic mental health counseling and criminal justice professions move toward an integrated model for treating criminal justice clients, those forensic mental health professionals that are skillful in working with offenders will be needing specific training in their chosen specialty area in order to manage the many co-morbid psychiatric disorders which many times co-occurs with the criminal justice client's criminal offense. Those mental health professionals working within the traditional mental health environment that are planning to become a forensic mental health professional will need to make major adjustments. The therapist or counselor working with a criminal justice client should be able to screen and assess for substance abuse problems, personality disorders, and other co-occurring disorders, and should be able to determine a primary, secondary, and tertiary diagnosis. To begin with, they must be knowledgeable of the psychosocial aspects of criminal behaviors as well as treatment modalities and treatment strategies.

Mental health professionals moving into the treatment of criminal justice clients, at a minimum, typically need training and supervision in:

"assessment" for substance abuse, personality disorders and other co-morbid psychiatric disorder that generally co-occur with criminal behaviors. Knowledge of risk assessment techniques to determine the "probability"

of re-offending, assessing client's individual treatment needs, and assessing treatment progress.

"therapy theories" which include cognitive-behavioral therapy, reality therapy, transactional analysis that pertain to a wide variety of specialties.

"group therapy" with knowledge of group developmental stages, screening clients for appropriateness to be placed in a group, client orientation, establishing boundaries, and utilizing group dynamics and specific techniques designed to confront the offender's criminal behaviors, distorted thinking errors and beliefs, identifying client risk factors, and relapse prevention planning.

"Supervision" which is important in skills and group training should be under the supervision of an experienced and skilled therapist. Supervision enable the therapist to obtain first hand experience, and assists in the better understanding of what is happening in the type of group they will eventually be leading. The supervisor should be knowledgeable and competent in the specialty area in which they are providing supervision. For example, domestic violence battery, substance abuse, sexual offending or general offending psychosocial dynamics.

"Legal Issues" are important for the forensic therapist to be aware of particularly with criminal justice clients because of the "limited confidentiality" issues inherent in the acceptance of criminal justice referrals, and the requirements of sharing assessment reports and keeping the courts apprised of the offender's progress. It is also important for the forensic therapist to know Federal regulations and State laws concerning "duty to warn"

requirements pertaining to child abuse, elder abuse, "commitment procedures" for psychiatric disorders, "HIV/AIDS," "adolescents," and "managed care," as well as the Federal confidentiality regulations, 42 C.F.R. Part 2 pertaining to Alcohol and drug abuse patient records.

Recovery and Relapse Prevention Planning

As we discussed briefly in chapter 6, the purpose of all criminal justice client groups, regardless of the offense they committed is for the offender to develop their relapse prevention plan. One of the group goals is the identification of each individual's pattern or cycle of criminal acting out. The philosophy of taking this particular approach is in the belief that an offender, regardless of their offense can experience what I refer to as "the tugs" to return to their previous criminal lifestyle and re-offend. The belief is that treatment can assist the offender in learning "how" to manage their tugs, but is not a cure of their "tugs" to return to their criminal lifestyle and re-offending.

The development of the offender's personalized relapse prevention plan is initiated after total group admission of and discussion of their criminal pattern of criminal acting out behaviors. This involves an examination of the progression from their first urge or tug, through all the cognitive steps that concluded in the criminal offense. During this process, the therapist assists the offender in fully understanding their offense patterns and cycle, as well as the specific distorted pre-offense thoughts, beliefs, feelings, and behaviors. Together, the therapist and offender identify the progressive and self-reinforcing nature of the pre-offense elements so the offender will recognize that their criminal acting out was not a spontaneous event, but rather a series of predictable thoughts, beliefs, feelings, and behaviors as well as their existing maintenance behaviors that makes them susceptible to re-offend. The cycle of distorted thinking, beliefs, and feelings is extremely difficult to break because it has become, for the offender, a habitual way of responding to their world that occurs almost without their awareness.

The relapse prevention plan examines and takes each step of the offender's offense cycle and creates alternate thoughts, beliefs, feelings, and behaviors as well as options and diversions designed to disrupt the offender's criminal thinking and the offense cycle. The relapse prevention plan is developed in a way so that it may be modified as new insights are gained during treatment. To be most effective, the relapse prevention plan should be developed with the offender's probation or parole agent's participation, and shared with others who support the offender's treatment and may be of assistance in the offender carrying out their plan.

Relapse among criminal justice clients is a constant safety concern for the community. However, the development of a relapse prevention plan reduces the risk of re-offending. Those who commit criminal acts with a co-occurring disorder such as antisocial personality disorder, substance abuse or a major affective disorder are at a higher risk for re-offending if they display little or no insight into the impact of their crimes or their co-occurring disorder.

Very much like any other problem or disorder, criminal behavior is a chronic relapsing condition with or without the presence of a comorbid psychiatric disorder. Given the chronic, recurrent nature of criminal behaviors by themselves, or those complicated by the presence of a psychiatric disorder and the longitudinal nature of recovery, relapse prevention for offenders with co-occurring disorders should be incorporated into all criminal justice treatment programs.

Research on Relapse Prevention

As McGovern, et al (2005), points out, research on substance abuse and relapse prevention is extensive; however, other studies have addressed relapse and relapse prevention among clients with co-occurring disorders. Goodwin, et al (1990), identifies the presence of a bi-polar disorder as a high-risk factor for relapse. Manic episodes and severe anxiety are to an exceptional degree, likely to result in relapse, Bradizza, et al, 2003. Other researchers have linked relapse to social pressures, Alverson, et al, 2001, for example, peer pressure to return to the use of drugs, or pressure to return to a criminal lifestyle, and yet other researchers have identified interpersonal stressors as being high-risk situations in relapse, Bradizza, et al, 1998. We can also include other common risk factors that we are familiar with that contribute to relapse, such as, inadequate housing, unemployment, low income, dysfunctional family system, or deprivation of other basic needs just to mention a few. However, Davis, et al, 2005, did a focus group analysis of recovering persons and discovered that those clients who prevented relapsing did so through the use of behavioral strategies to avoid their high-risk situations and focusing on healthy behaviors such as attending dual diagnosis, or dual recovery self help groups, and relying on spirituality as used in alcoholics anonymous, and being involved in meaningful activities, and developing meaningful goals prevented their relapse.

Developing the
Relapse Prevention
Plan (RPP)

They're a number of formats for developing a relapse prevention plan (RPP); however, most employ the following elements:

1. *Identify high-risk situations*: Symptoms of relapse are generally experienced by exposure to certain people, places, things, or events. For example, a criminal justice client that was convicted of burglary numerous times is likely to experience tugs if they found an open window while walking down an alley or a recovering addict may experience tugs to relapse back into substance abuse if they accidentally ran into a drug dealer they once purchased drugs from. These types of situations are referred to as "triggers," tugs, or high-risk situations. They are referred to as such because they indicate a high probability of the client re-offending based on past experience. Relapse by criminal justice clients are generally due to either interpersonal conflict, negative peer pressure, or poor emotional management skills. Criminal justice clients while in treatment should closely monitor their own behav-

ior, being aware of when they are exposed to a high-risk situation, what symptoms they are experiencing, and what was going on immediately prior to them experiencing the tugs. In the Gorski, 1990 model, which can also be applied to general criminal justice clients as well as substance abusers, the client does a self-assessment of the presenting problem, and their past criminal history to determine the past causes of relapse.

2. *Developing strategies to respond to high-risk situations*: Once the client identifies their high-risk situations, they begin the process of exploring new ways of coping with the high-risk situation. Education and information sharing is useful as to what causes relapse, and what the client can do to prevent it. Education and information sharing is good; however, individualized strategies must be developed by the client that works for them to increase the probability of success. The tugs to return to what was familiar to the client is powerful. (Marlatt, 1985) defines what I refer to as the "tugs" as cravings for addicts as the level of need for the positive affects the individual expects as a result of use and an urge as the want to engage in use to satisfy a craving. The best strategy is to not expose one self to a high-risk situation, which may include avoiding certain people, places, and events. Avoidance is a great strategy to use, for example, the client that was convicted of burglary that encountered the open window in an alley can avoid the tugs by immediately walking away from

the exposed window, or the substance abuser avoiding a party where they know other drug users will be attending. Developing strategies for unavoidable triggers such as "happy hours at bars" are generally skills that must be learned and practiced regularly in order to work. Some of these strategies may include calling a friend or counselor, going to an AA, NA, or OA meeting, using meditation techniques, progressive muscle relaxation, deep breathing, praying, etc., any technique that will assist in refocusing, reframing, positive self talk, cognitive restructuring, maintaining a journal, or avoiding a situation can be utilized to deal with high-risk situations.

3. *Developing a pro-social support system*: Support systems are most effective when they involve family and friends who care about the client in treatment. Other sources are also good such as AA, NA, or OA if the offender is estranged from family and friends. It is advisable that family or significant others be involved if available in the treatment process so everyone fully understands the offender's goals, and is aware of the warning signs for relapse. The use of support groups are important during the offender's recovery; however, they are not designed to address the offender's core psychological issues which may cause a relapse that requires attention of a licensed mental health professional.

4. *Being prepared for the tugs and possible relapse*: Relapse rates are very high among criminal justice clients with or without comorbidity.

The client must be aware that even if they are doing what they believe is their best; they may experience a lapse (an occurrence of a thought, belief, feeling or behavior) or a relapse (the return to a previous level of thinking, feeling and behaving). It is important to make the offender aware of these possibilities, and that a lapse or even a relapse does not mean that they are not getting well and they're notfailures in order to avoid them giving up completely if or when it does occur.

The above elements are fairly common to most relapse prevention programs; however, a relapse prevention plan can also be designed to include co-occurring disorders such as substance abuse, personality disorders, or anxiety disorders. Relapse prevention is an essential component of recovery since the return to an antisocial lifestyle following treatment is a common occurrence. Although there are different relapse prevention models, it is essential to develop a cognitive-behavioral relapse prevention plan with criminal justice clients because of their distorted thoughts, feelings, and beliefs that need to be restructured in order to change their behaviors and prevent relapse.

Cognitive-Behavioral RP Plan

The cognitive-behavioral RPP model for criminal justice clients is the most effective RPP model because its focus is on increasing the offender's knowledge about their high-risk situations and developing cognitive-behavioral coping strategies to deal with them. Developing and implementing a cognitive-behavioral relapse prevention plan involves systematic practice (rehearsal) of the coping strategies the offender developed to deal with the identified high-risk situations. The following examples may be helpful:

1. For those criminal justice clients having difficulty identifying their high-risk situations, the therapist can encourage them to seek input from their family, significant other, friends, or other supportive people. The therapist can assist the offender role-play with specific questions they will ask someone to assist in identifying their high-risk situations.

2. If the offender decides that decreasing stress should be part of their RPP, the therapist can assist them in role-playing muscle relaxation or deep breathing stress reduction techniques.

3. If calling a friend, family member or other person is part of the RPP, they can role-play what they will say if they need to make that call.

4. The therapist assisting in the development of the RPP can follow up with homework assignments such as:

    a) Discussing with people that are supportive of them about their high-risk situations.

    b) Discuss with supporters about early warning signs of relapse they have observed in the past.

    c) Asking those that are supportive of them

to play a specific role in their relapse prevention plan.

d) Providing their supporters with a copy of their RPP.

e) Attending support group meetings.

Sometimes the criminal justice client with a long history of living an antisocial lifestyle may report that they can't identify their high-risk situations. When this mental block does occur, it may be useful for the offender to discuss with those that are supportive of their treatment, what they may remember and be able to identify. If no one is able to assist the client, the therapist may want to help the client to at least identify the earliest symptoms they experience prior to committing a crime.

When discussing with the offender the possibility of a lapse or relapse, they may experience unpleasant memories and become agitated thinking about them. The therapist at this point can focus the discussion on identifying important information for the future. It is also useful to point out to the offender their strengths in managing their antisocial behavior as well as any co-occurring disorder, and commend them for their participation in developing a relapse prevention plan for improving their future. Many times, by the therapist discussing any unpleasant memories that are identified may be very helpful, because the offender may benefit from developing a new perspective on their high-risk situations, and become even more motivated to identify them.

Characteristics of Recovering Offenders

I am often asked by students, trainees, and mental health practitioners, "How do you really know if a criminal justice client is in recovery?" My response every time is that we don't know for certain, but there are observable behaviors that may indicate the offender is recovering. It doesn't matter whether we believe what we are observing is real or not, we must give the offender the benefit of the doubt unless we have unambiguous proof it is not real, for example, a positive urinalysis for a illegal substance, a failed polygraph, information from the offender's family or significant others, employers, violation of probation or parole, or a re-arrest.

A close colleague of mine (Carich, 1997) has identified thirty-three characteristics of recovering sex offenders of which many also apply to other offenders as well. The characteristics that do apply to all criminal justice clients include:

"More honesty." The client stops denying responsibility for their criminal lifestyle choices, and is more intimate with others. Is willing to confront other group members on their criminal thinking when identified.

"Level of entitlement" appears to be within normal limits. Has no unreasonable expectations from others.

"Client appears less narcissistic" as evidenced by their realistic explanation of their abilities, accomplishments, and expectations.

"Expresses their feelings appropriately" by identifying and getting in touch with their feelings and managing their emotions.

"Stopped being hostile" toward others as evidenced by

their use of learned social skills, problem solving techniques, and their ability to resolve interpersonal conflicts without becoming angry or threatening.

"*Displays empathy toward others*" as evidenced by their ability to place themselves in their victims, and other group members, positions by identifying with their feelings.

"*Behavior is consistent*" as evidenced by prosocial attitudes and behaviors.

"*Client works on long-term goals*" in group and outside group on their own time.

"*Client is aware of their criminal behavior cycle*" as evidenced by their sharing details in group and with their therapist.

"*Client is aware of their high-risk situations*" as evidenced by their identifying and sharing their high-risk situations in group.

"*Client has developed new coping skills*" to effectively deal with their high-risk situations when faced with them.

"*Client is able to explain the psychosocial dynamics of their offending*" taking full responsibility without blaming others, society, the courts, or their past experiences.

"*Client has developed a positive support system*" as evidenced by their support group attendance such as AA, NA, or OA, and the development of new positive peer friendships.

"*Client has stopped living a secret life*" as evidenced by their openly sharing with others their past offenses and offense details.

"*Client has developed a sense of spiritualism*" as evidenced by their believing in a power higher than themselves.

"*Client's self-esteem improves*" as evidenced by their appearance, how they refer to themselves, and their being proud of their accomplishments in treatment.

"*Client's thinking is less distorted*" as observed by their being less confused, and more open and honest with others.

"*Leisure time.*" Most criminal justice clients have had only one leisure time activity, looking for and finding trouble. Criminal justice clients become easily bored when they are not out doing their usual thing … getting into trouble. Clients that are working toward recovery find pro-social activities to participate in such as, joining a gymnasium, attending support group meetings, joining a basketball, baseball, or softball team.

"*Social and communication skills.*" Most criminal justice clients lack social and communication skills because they never had to rely on them. Most of their relationships have been with peers that shared antisocial attitudes, which created a social network for them. When in the process of recovery, the therapist should be able to observe improved listening skills, the client engaging in small talk, and openly sharing information about themselves.

"*Self Care.*" Most criminal justice clients lack good hygiene and may appear unkempt or even dirty. They simply may not know how to practice good hygiene, how to dress, or how to eat because of their low self-esteem, poor-self image, and feelings of no self-worth.

During the recovery process, the therapist should be able to observe changes in their self care as their social skills improve.

Some interventions you may want to utilize in assessing the criminal justice client's recovery may include, "What do you think you have learned in treatment?" "What do you still need to work on?" "What is most problematic for you to work on?" "What are your future goals?" "How do you think your life is going to be better if you stop offending?" "How far do you think you are in your recovery?" "What other problems do you think you may have that will be a deterrent to your full recovery?" "What else are you willing to give up to assure your full recovery?"

As important as it is to assess your client's progress as they work toward their recovery, it is also equally important to possess the skills to detect when a client is conning, manipulating, or faking their progress. Some of the most common characteristics that I have identified that indicate the client may be faking include:

1. *"Not focusing"* and jumping from one topic to another in an attempt to avoid what may be a real issue.

2. *"Client is non-committal"* and responds to the therapists interventions with, I don't know, could be, maybe, or possibly, avoiding answering "yes" or "no."

3. *"Over adapting"* to everything the therapist says, attempts to figure out what the therapist wants to hear.

4. *"Question avoidance" by* answering questions

with a question, or redefining the question to fit their frame of reference.

5. *"Client avoids eye contact"* with the therapist. Looks at the floor, wall, or ceiling when responding to the therapist.

6. *"Denial."* Client continues to deny either the existence, severity, or solvability of their problem as well as their ability to solve their problem.

7. *"Minimization."* The client minimizes their criminal behavior or substance abuse.

8. *"Blaming."* Client has excuses for everything that has gone wrong for them in life, and blames others for all their misfortunes.

9. *"Redefining."* Client attempts to redefine the therapist's interventions, for example:

> Therapist: Jason, you were convicted of child molestation. Is that correct?
>
> Client: That's what they said, "but she really asked me to touch her."

10. *"Avoidance of feelings."* The client avoids identifying and getting in touch with their feelings and demonstrates poor emotional control. Generally, the client's affect is flat, dulled, or very bland.

Phases of Recovery from Criminal Behaviors

Recovery from criminal acting out behavior is defined as the offender maintaining their social control and refraining from offending. Gaining social control and maintaining abstinence requires the development of skills, change of attitude, and commitment to a pro-social lifestyle. Every offender is a unique being with their own characteristics, and yet, most of them share similar thoughts, beliefs, feelings, behaviors, wants, and needs. Many offenders have "hit their bottom" long before they were mandated to treatment by the courts, and have been sick and tired of being sick and tired for a long time. When offered an opportunity to change, the criminal justice client many times appears suspicious, cautious, and even resistant. However, the largest majority of them will eventually begin to comply, and begin the recovery process. During my career working this special need population, I have identified 4 phases of recovery from living a criminal lifestyle as discussed below.

Phase 1. Compliance

During the first phase of recovery, the offender is reluctant to participate fully. They will display their antisocial thinking, feeling, beliefs, and behaviors, believing they are vulnerable because they were forced into treatment. Some offenders during the early stages of phase I may even become emotionally distressed. During this early stage, there is little or no cognitive recognition into their criminal thinking, feeling, and behaviors. The therapist during this phase should focus on the issue of the client's lack of social control, and obtaining a commitment from the client that they maintain social control, and will not criminally act during the course of treatment. Once the client agrees, the therapist should have the client sign a social control contract to that effect. A sample social control contract that you may want to consider using is available in the appendix of this book. By the client signing the social control contract they are agreeing to comply. What is meant by compliance during this early stage is the client agreeing to the basic concept of abstaining from criminal acting out behaviors as being an essential part of recovery.

Once the client becomes compliant, the next step is getting the client to accept responsibility for their criminal behaviors, and how their behaviors have affected them personally, their family, children, friends, and the community. Now that the client has taken responsibility, they must also begin the process of identifying their cycle of offending. While the client is exploring their criminal behavior cycles, the therapist should also be confronting and restructuring the offense specific cognitive distortions, beliefs, and feelings the client uses to avoid the guilt of committing a crime. The goal is for the client to gain awareness of their criminal behavior patterns and the thoughts, feelings, and beliefs, which accompany them.

During Phase I the client should also be learning new social skills and be in empathy training. The newly learned social skills and empathy should be observable in their group interactions, and feedback from family or others. The client should be showing empathy to others in their group by relating to their problems and feelings they are experiencing.

Phase II Contemplation

During this stage of recovery, the client cognitively recognizes their criminal acting out cycle, and begins to develop self-management skills, moving out of being chained to their problems into solutions. The client is less defensive and has gained a greater sense of emotional and personal identity. The client during this stage is beginning to trust themselves to solve their problems, and begins to trust others as well.Along with the development of self-management skills, the client begins to restructure their lifestyle by attending AA, NA, or OA meetings, making new friends, and internalizing pro-social community values. The client continues working on identifying their high-risk factors and develops coping skills to deal with them.

Phase III Motivation

During Phase III the client is beginning to reap the rewards of restructuring their lifestyle and is highly motivated to maintain their social control and not re-offend. The client during this phase of their recovery is active in group both receiving feedback, and providing feedback to others. Clinical core issues continue to be worked on and resolved without resistance. The client continues going to their support group meetings, maintaining and updating their relapse prevention plan coping techniques. The client makes obvious their high motivation and desire to change their lives.

Phase IV Maintenance

During Phase IV, the client continues being highly motivated to maintain their social control by continuing their relapse prevention strategies. The client acknowledges that their recovery has become possible because they stopped denying the existence and severity of their problems making them responsible for solving them. The client at this point has moved through their negativeness and hostility into acceptance, recovery, and voluntarily seeking a pro-social lifestyle.

COURT ORDERED

COUNSELING: AN ETHICAL DILEMMA

Court ordered counseling for criminal justice clients presents the forensic therapist with ethical concerns related to dual relationships, informed consent, and confidentiality. As I mentioned earlier in this text, the courts refer criminal justice clients for treatment, sometimes to therapists who have little or no experience working with offenders and who are also unaware of the ethical implications of such referrals. The acceptance of criminal justice clients into counseling programs has been rapidly increasing since the 1990s and has been referred to as either "mandated treatment" or "coerced treatment" by therapists and agencies accepting them. Therapists accepting criminal justice referrals are also expected and required to resolve these ethical dilemmas, many times by breaching long-established mental health principles such as confidentiality. Resolution of ethical standards within court mandated counseling programs has, up to the time of this writing been at the very best difficult. It's even more difficult to resolve the many ethical questions related to court mandated treatment of offenders, especially when some programs for general and sexual offenders require that the offender involuntarily participate in the program to either avoid incarceration or to complete probation or parole requirements, regardless of the offender's lack of interest, or be referred back to court for non-compliance which makes it even more difficult to be reconciled with long-established mental health ethics. To even further the problem, many sex offender and general offender programs require that the offender must admit to their guilt in order to participate in the program. The dilemma then is does this requirement violate the offender's Fifth Amendment right against self-incrimination? Whether the courts agree that the Fifth Amendment protects an already convicted and sentenced offender from having to admit guilt mostly depends upon how the offender pled at trial. If the offender pled guilty to the crime they are charged with, they waive certain constitutional rights, including the right against required self-incrimination.

Offender satisfaction with the program they have been court ordered to attend is generally ignored and considered to be immaterial, although it is recognized that promoting an offender's self-esteem is important in reducing recidivism (Marshall et al, 1999). Program effectiveness most times focuses on such criteria as successfully completing the program, delays in re-offending, remaining drug free during treatment, and decreased cost to the community. A thorough investigation and evaluation of the ethical dilemmas faced by the forensic therapist is beyond the scope of this chapter. However, we will explore the most obvious dilemmas that cause liability concerns faced by the forensic therapist such as informed consent, confidentiality, and dual relationships.

Informed Consent

It is generally accepted in the mental health profession that a client's informed written consent is required prior to being treated. There are several requirements that are essential for a legally acceptable consent to participate in treatment. First, the individual's intelligence and mental status must be adequate to allow them to fully understand to what they are consenting. Second, the individual must be fully informed and explained to in detail of any risks and benefits involved in their treatment or program, as well as any alternatives. The third requirement for informed consent is that the individual's choice be voluntary and not coerced. This third requirement seems to be the most critical factor in assessing the informed consent of criminal justice clients. If consent is given because the offender is court mandated, rather than indicating a voluntary willingness to participate in treatment, the offender's informed written consent may be because the offender believes that their participation is required as an alternative to incarceration, or a condition of probation or parole. Although this sounds as if the offender's consent may be involuntary and could be legally scrutinized it is seldom raised. If no harm has occurred, and perhaps the offender benefitted, the likelihood of a lawsuit against the therapist or program is reasonably small.

In defense of mandated treatment and the offender not having a choice of the type of therapy or who their therapist will be, there is empirical evidence that therapists and programs utilizing particular treatments such as cognitive-behavior therapy results in lower re-offending rates (Marshall, et al, 1999), even though such practices may infringe on the client's rights, and the therapist's code of ethics. Here comes the dilemma, "treatment of offenders, and particularly sex offenders, in order for treatment to be effective must be involuntary." Offenders, when ordered into treatment, are more likely to persevere in treatment than offenders who volunteer for treatment who generally have a worse outcome than the involuntary offender (Salter, 1988). In addition, many prominent researchers in the field advocate for mandated treatment. (Marshall, 1999) advocates that such interventions should combine sensible treatment with incarceration stating: "These men knowingly engage in behaviors that are unlawful, as evidenced by the fact that they take great care to avoid detection and by the fact that most act to prevent their victims from reporting the offense, clear feedback from society, by way of a prison sentence, makes it apparent to these men, as it does to all offenders, that their abusive actions are not acceptable."

Most general offender, domestic violence batterers, substance abuse, and sex offender programs are part of the punishment that is ordered by the court, which requires the therapist to accept a value system, which is inconsistent with traditional codes of practice employed by a mental health practitioner. The primary purpose of treatment is not what is in the best interest of the offender, but is rather, the protection of the community. For the most part, forensic therapists treating any court ordered offender is practicing in an ethical void because they are required as part of good clinical practice treating offenders to violate ethical principles (Deisler, 2004). Most therapists treating offenders are firmly committed to the good of society rather than the welfare of the client, and in spite of all the ethical dilemmas, they make the programs work, which is evidenced by a drop in recidivism rates for offenders treated compared to offenders who are untreated. As pointed out by (Marshall, et al, 1999), such successes have reduced the suffering of potential victims, the community, and savings in the costs to criminal justice, the offender, and their families.

In short, an offender's informed consent must be in writing and must be voluntarily given by the offender who is "substantially capable to understand all the information specified on the consent form." At a minimum, the form must contain:

1. Name of the person whose assessment report or treatment record is being disclosed.

2. The purpose and need for the disclosure.

3. The specific information being disclosed.

4. The time period during which the consent is effective.

5. The date on which the consent was signed.

6. The signature of the criminal justice client giving consent.

Most state laws also require that the consent form must also include a statement of the offender's right to copies of the disclosed information during their treatment and after termination. A copy of the consent form must be provided to the offender, and one copy in the offender's treatment record. The offender must be advised that they have the right to refuse consent, and may withdraw their consent at any time.

HIV/AIDS

Many criminal justice clients have engaged in behaviors that put them at risk to contract HIV/AIDS such as prostitution, promiscuousness, and intravenous drug use. As a result, the forensic therapist must possess a broad knowledge of HIV infection and AIDS. It is the responsibility of the therapist to know the laws within the state they are practicing related to HIV and AIDS. Confidentiality laws dealing with offenders who have HIV or AIDS are multifaceted and state governments often have difficulty balancing need-to-know situations related to HIV/AIDS with the principle of confidentiality. If the therapist is practicing within a state with no specific legislation, protection of the offenders HIV/AIDS records may be provided by medical records statutes. However, in most states, the sharing of information related to an offender's positive HIV/AIDS test or status may result in a malpractice lawsuit.

Limited Confidentiality

Criminal justice clients referred by the courts for outpatient treatment are not voluntary. The court, when referring the offender to treatment, generally establishes a set of conditions specifying certain limitations of treatment and other aspects of the offender's daily life, which is imposed by the referring court (Meichenbaum and Turk, 1987). Communication between the court and the treating program is essential for effective treatment of the criminal justice client. The sharing of information regarding the offender's treatment progress or lack of progress, as well as treatment needs and risk factors are critical for the community management of offenders and public safety. This approach serves both the offender's therapeutic needs and public protection. The failure to share the criminal justice client's treatment information with the courts could have negative effects for the offender, victim, community, treatment program, and the therapist. Without the sharing of information about the offender's treatment progress, risk factors, and their behaviors, it is unlikely that either will be served satisfactorily (Petrila and Sadoff, 1992).

The issue of the criminal justice client's limited confidentiality should be addressed prior to the beginning of treatment. The treatment contract must state clearly that there will be on-going communications between the program, therapist, and the courts on treatment progress, assessments, behavior and identified risk factors in order to avoid any misunderstandings during the course of treatment. The treatment contract should be signed by the therapist, the client, and a witness. The criminal justice client receives one copy, the court/probation/parole agent one copy, and one copy placed in the offender's medical file. You may want to consider using the sample informed consent contract in appendix A of this book.

Dual Relationships

Dual relationships have been the leading cause of malpractice lawsuits in the counseling profession since the early 1990s. A dual relationship exists whenever a therapist interrelates with their client in any capacity other than therapist and client. For example, being a client's business partner, legal advisor, consultant, having a sexual relationship with a current or former client, lending money, borrowing money from a client, bartering therapy services for discounts, goods, legal or professional services are all considered having a dual relationship with the client. Having a dual relationship with a client seriously distorts the therapist-client therapeutic relationship, and limits the therapeutic handling of the various therapy variables such as transference.

Most dual relationships don't just happen; they are usually very subtle and gradual and could be the consequence of the therapist's inattention to the therapeutic relationship. Avoiding a dual relationship with a criminal justice client requires strict boundaries because of their character pathology and tendency to con and manipulate others. The boundaries are the rules that clearly define the therapist-client roles and should not be compromised.

If at any time during the therapeutic relationship with a criminal justice client you begin to suspect that you are being drawn into a dual relationship, or that one has already been established, consider the following courses of action:

1. Act immediately. Confront the client with what you believe is interfering with the therapeutic relationship. Be specific and work to resolve the issue with the client about the precise dynamics of the dual relationship.

2. Document in the client's medical record all interactions in detail on how you think the client was attempting to establish a dual relationship with you.

3. Seek consultation with a supervisor or colleague on how to end a dual relationship with the least amount of harm to the client and

yourself.

4. With the client, yourself and your supervisor attempt to devise a mutually agreeable solution to restore a healthy therapeutic relationship.

5. If attempts to resolve the issue have failed, consider transferring the client to another therapist, or terminating the client as a last resort.

Malpractice Suits

The exposure to a possible professional liability suit is extremely high when treating the criminal justice client for a few reasons. First, most criminal justice clients that have an antisocial, narcissistic, or paranoid personality disorder are extremely manipulative and very adamant in wanting to figure out "how do I get myself out of here." They have heard from the street "grapevine" that it has been successful in the past to file a suit against the treatment program, which will result in their getting out of treatment, and in many cases even off probation. So guess what? They look for things they can sue for such as:

1. Lack of confidentiality.

2. Faulty chain of custody on urinalysis tests.

3. Failure to get releases of information from group members to video a group session, or to allow an outsider to observe the group.

4. Their treatment is different from what they agreed to in the treatment contract.

5. Mental, emotional, or psychological abuse as

a result of the therapist's use of confrontation, interventions, home work assignments, AA, NA or OA attendance.

6. They are required to pay a fee for their involuntary treatment.

7. The therapist sexually harassed them.

8. The therapist is prejudiced and discriminated against their sex, color, religion, sexual orientation, etc.

9. Client was placed in a mixed group of males and females and as a result became involved with another client and got pregnant.

10. Dual relationships.

These are just a few of the attempts that have been made to discredit treatment programs by criminal justice clients in the past. The best advice I can give you on how to avoid a malpractice suit is to avoid them by assuring that your treatment contract is thorough and clearly delineates every component of treatment. Even if you're a competent practitioner who performs in a manner consistent with the standards of your profession, you may still have to deal with difficult situations and unhappy criminal justice clients. Following are some tips for avoiding a professional liability suit that are fairly easy and should be incorporated into your practice with criminal justice clients:

1. Be certain that you clearly establish and define the therapist/client relationship and boundaries. Be aware of and avoid dual relationships.

2. Be certain to follow appropriate chain of cus-

tody when taking a urinalysis test from a client.

3. Be certain that your record keeping is accurate, thorough and up to date (American Psychological Association, 1995).

4. Don't mix male and female criminal justice clients in the same group.

5. Ensure that you have the proper education, training, experience and supervision to treat the criminal justice population.

6. When a client does complain about something, respond empathically.

7. Consult your professional association, or a colleague with any questions you may have about ethics or legal issues.

8. Don't utilize high confrontational techniques that may be construed as being abusive.

9. Avoid being alone with certain clients to avoid allegations of sexual impropriety by having another therapist present or keeping the door open.

10. Be cautious with clients who have a tendency for bringing legal actions.

11. Be familiar with your state licensing board's code of ethics for your profession (Corey and Callahan, 2002) (Lowenberg, Dolgoff, and Harrington, 2000).

12. Do not give clients legal advice.

Assessment Reports

The essentials of an assessment report may vary, depending on the legal and forensic issues at hand as well as the requirements of the court of jurisdiction. The guidelines of the report should be established and agreed upon prior to you doing the assessment to assure it will meet the needs of the court. The following headings are generally included in most criminal forensic assessment reports:

Title–Use the legal title of the case you are writing your report on (e.g., State of Indiana v. Jason K. Norstar) along with the case docket number and name of the court.

Reason for Referral–State the reason the defendant was referred to you (e.g., risk assessment, personality assessment after client was arrested and charged with the crime of burglary, child molestation, etc).

Client History–Include previous arrests, convictions, incarcerations, probations, paroles,mental health counseling, medical history, medications, family history, marital status, number, and ages of any dependents, alcohol/drug history, military history, educational history, employment history, present employment status, etc.

Sources of Information–Official records, client interviews, etc.

TestsAdministered–(for example) Minnesota Multiphasic Personality Inventory (MMPI) Personality Assessment Inventory (PAI) Static 99 Vermont Assessment of Sex Offender Risk (VASOR)

Test Results–Describe the relevant data from each examination you administered as well as conclusions that the data supports.

Conclusions and Recommendations–State your recommendations as suggestions rather than a decision about what should happen along with a sound rationale (e.g., based upon Jason's long history of outpatient treatment failures for sexual assault as well as his failures to comply with community supervision requirements, Jason may be best served within a structured environment at the Midway Correctional Institute which also has a sex offender treatment program).

Diagnostic Impression–Be certain to use the DSM IV-TR five Axis diagnoses.

Date and Signature–The report should include your signature and the date it was completed.

Before submitting your report to the court of jurisdiction, review it and be certain that it is credible, impartial, thorough, well documented and meets both clinical and legal standards. Ask yourself, is the language clear and concise? Does the case, client's history, and test data support your recommendations? Do you have your facts, opinions, and recommendations differentiated? Does your report look and sound professional including format, contents, grammar, and spelling?

APPENDIX A

Treatment Contract

(Appendix A or C can be used according to program needs)

I, _____, hereby enter into a voluntary agreement with_____

_____, to allow their staff to provide me with a specialized treatment group for my criminal behavior. I understand and agree to the following conditions regarding my treatment:

1. What I say and hear in treatment remains confidential.

2. I will be on time for all sessions and stay for the entire session.

3. I will be active in group sharing my problems, providing feed back to others, and confronting others in a respectful manner when appropriate.

4. I will take responsibility for my criminal behaviors, and discuss my offenses openly and honestly.

5. I will remain alcohol and drug free, and fully understand that I will be required to submit to a urinalysis as requested by my counselor, and if positive, I will be terminated from treatment and referred back to court/ probation/parole.

6. I will submit to a polygraph examination when requested, and if I refuse, I will be referred back to court/probation/parole.

7. I will complete in a timely manner all homework or other group assignments that are provided me.

8. I will not threaten others verbally, physically or psychologically.

9. I fully understand that I am responsible for my treatment fees, and that all fees' must be paid on time as delineated in the agencies financial agreement.

10. I also agree to the following special conditions at the suggestion of staff or myself:

A) _____

B) _____

C) _____

D) _____

E) _____

In exchange for my agreeing to the above conditions, my therapist will agree to Provide:

1. Provide group, individual, family, educational sessions as delineated in my TX plan.

2. Provide all materials and learning tools relevant to my therapy.

3. Provide adequate meeting space.

4. To be available to discuss issues/concerns with family and myself.

5. Provide information pertaining to my treatment progress to:

A) _____

B) _____

C) _____

D) _____

E) _____

6. To attend court proceedings as necessary.

7. To provide feedback on the results of evaluations and progress in therapy.

8. To confront, challenge and support me in my quest for growth and change.

I have read this treatment contract and fully understand its contents, and I agree to them. I fully understand that failure to keep this contract may or will result in my being terminated and being referred back to: _____

_____

_____

_____

_____

Client: _____   Date: _____

Therapist: _____   Date: _____

Therapist: _____   Date: _____

Witness: _____   Date: _____

Judge/probation officer/parole agent:

_____   Date: _____

APPENDIX B

Social Control Contract

1. If and when I get an urge or thought to commit a criminal offense, I will immediately *stop* and review my copy of the *Offense Prevention Plan*. I will think over the following: Having an urge or thought to commit a criminal offense *does not mean* my treatment is not working, or that I am hopeless, or a loser. It *does not mean* I have lost control. It *does not mean* I have to commit an offense. *I don't have to* give in to my urges to act out ... *I am in control* . What has happened that caused me to have these thoughts? How can I cope with the stress right now? What can I use that I learned in therapy right now? Who will I call and talk to if I need to? If I am still having problems overcoming my urge to act out, I will call my therapist, probation/parole agent, or call a friend. Therapist: (000)

000–0000 _____

Friend: (000) 000-0000 _____

Probation/parole: (000) 000-0000_____

I fully understand that *violation of this social control contract* will be reported to my probation or parole agent and may result in termination from the treatment pro-

gram and/or may result in a breach of my probation/
parole conditions

Client: _____ Date: _____

Therapist: _____ Date: _____

Therapist: _____ Date: _____

Probation/Parole Agent: _____

Date: _____

Appendix C

Treatment Contract and Informed Consent
Criminal Justice Referral

You, _____(Clients name)_____have been referred to_____(Name of agency)_____ by the_____(Name of court)_____as a condition of your probation or conditional release for_____ Counseling Assessment)_____.

Confidentiality

The strict principles of confidentiality and privilege do not apply under the present circumstances. The program/therapist is also required by law to report any incidences of child abuse, elder abuse, or threats of harm to another. The therapist is also required to share the following information *checked below* to:

Name: _____

Name: _____

Name: _____

Name: _____

1. Assessment results_____

2. Urinalysis test results_____

3. Polygraph test results_____

4. Treatment progress reports _____

5. Treatment plan _____

6. Progress notes _____

7. Termination report _____

8. Other_____(write in)

9. Other_____(write in)

10. Other_____(write in)

Other information, which may be shared, includes any statements made by you, tape recordings, diaries, workbooks, homework assignments, correspondence, photographs, and observations.

I _____ (Client Name)_____ understand that I may choose to refuse treatment and be returned to my referral source, and if I accept treatment I may be required to participate in one or more of the following activities while a client here at_____(Agency name)_____; Assessment, Treatment planning, Psychoeducational groups/classes, Individual therapy, Family/couples therapy, Group therapy, Anger management sessions, Conflict resolution sessions, Random urinalysis testing, Random polygraph testing, Support group attendance, Relapse prevention planning, Other_____

I fully understand that I will be required to attend on time all sessions scheduled for me, and that I am financially responsible for my assessment/treatment fees as agreed upon in my financial agreement in the amount of_____ per week/biweekly/monthly. I fully understand and I have been explained to that failure to participate in my program, violation of program rules, or to pay my fees may result in my termination and referral back to my referral source. I fully understand that the program rules are as follows:

1. No violence or threats of violence against other program participants or program staff.

2. No use of alcohol or other substances while in treatment.

3. Attend all sessions on time unless excused.

4. Pay all fees as agreed upon within my financial agreement.

5. Fully participate in my program and follow all treatment instructions.

6. Other_____

7. Other_____

In turn for my program participation, I understand that my therapist will:

1. Provide appropriate professional space for my sessions.

2. Provide assessments, individual, group or family/couples therapy as delineated in my treatment plan or as may be required.

3. Attend court hearings on my behalf as required.

4. Be professionally qualified to provide services to me.

5. Consult with my attorney as may be required.

6. Share with me the contents of any reports being sent to my referral source.

Your signature below indicates that (1) you have received a copy of, read, fully understand, and will abide by the program rules and procedures; (2) you are waiving privilege with respect to my sharing with the above checked persons any information in my files concerning you; (3) you are authorizing the release by me of information to the courts, probation officer, parole agent, and other parties to which I have been directed to release by the court.

Client's Name	Client's Signature	Date Signed
Witness Name	Witness Signature	Date Signed
Therapist's Name	Therapist's Signature	Date Signed

BIBLIOGRAPHY

Chapter 1

American Psychiatric Association. (1994). *Diagnostic and Statistical Manual of Mental Disorders, 4th ed.* Washington, DC: American Psychiatric Press. Cleckley, H. (1964). *The Mask of Insanity*, St. Louis: Mosby. Craft, Stephenson, Granger. (1964). *A Controlled Trial of Authoritarian and Self Governing Regimes with Adolescent Psychopaths.* The American Journal of *Orthopsychiatry*. Deisler, F. J. (2002). The Personality Disorders. *The Forensic Therapist Magazine, Volume 2, Issue 3.*Hare, R.D. (1993). *Without Conscience: The Disturbing World of the Psychopaths among Us.* New York, N.Y, Pocket Books. Lykken, David, T. (1995). *The Antisocial Personality Disorder.* University of Minnesota. McCall, Raymond, J. (1975). *The Varieties of Abnormality.* Charles C. Thomas. Parsian, A., and Cloninger, C.R. (1991). *Genetics of High Risk Populations.* Addiction and Recovery. Regier, D.A., Farmer, M.E., Et al. (1990). *Comorbidity of Mental Disorders with Alcohol and Drug Abuse.* Journal of the American Medical Association. Samenow, S. (1998). *Straight Talk about Criminals.* Jason Aronson, Inc. Stout, M.L., and Mintz, L.B. (1996). *Differences among*

Nonclinical College Women with Alcoholic Mothers, Alcoholic Fathers, and Nonalcoholic Parents. Journal of Counseling Psychology. Toth, M.K., (1990). *Understanding and Treating Conduct Disorders.* Pro-Ed.

Chapter 2

Abel, Gene. (2004). *The Abel Assessment for Sexual Interest-2.* Abel Behavioral Institute, Atlanta, GA. Andrews and Bonta, et al. (1998). *Does Correctional Treatment Work? A Clinically Relevant and Psychologically Informed Meta Analysis.* Criminology 28: 369–404. Anglin, M.D., Et al. (1989). *Pretreatment Characteristics and Treatment Performance of Legally Coerced Admissions.* Criminology, 27, 537–557.Campbell, J. (1995). *Criminal Justice Assessment: For Mental Health Professionals.* Forensic Publications, New York, N.Y. Carich, M.S., and Adkerson, D. (1995). *Adult Sexual Offender Assessment Packet.* Brandon, Vermont: The Safer Society Press. Deisler, F.J. (2003). *Understanding and Treating the Sociopathic Client.* Armadillo, Texas: Armadillo Publishing. Deisler, F.J. (2004). *Adult Reoffense Risk Assessment.* Fort Wayne, Indiana: National Association of Forensic Counselors, Inc. Goldcamp, J.S., and Weiland, D. (1993). *Assessing the impact of Dade County's Felony Drug Court.* Washington, DC: National Institute of Justice. Hanson, R.K. (1998). *Evaluation of Manitoba's Secondary Risk Assessment.* Unpublished manuscript. Hanson, K., Thornton, D. (1999). *The Static 99.* Solicitor General Canada: Ottawa, Canada. Hare, R. (1991). *Psychopathy Check List.* Matuschka, E. (1985). *Treatment, Outcomes, and clinical Evaluation.* In T.E. Bratter and G.G. Forest (Eds.). *Alcoholism and Substance Abuse:*

Strategies for Clinical Intervention. New York: The Free Press. McGrath, R.J., and Cumming, G. (2003). *Sex Offender Treatment Needs and Progress Scale.* Research version: Vermont Department of Corrections. McGrath and Hoke. (1994). *Vermont Assessment of Sex Offender Needs.* Developmental Study. McGrath and Hoke. (1995). *Vermont Assessment of Sex Offender Risk.* Vermont Department of Corrections. Miller, G.A. (1997). *The Substance Abuse Subtle Screening Inventory-3 Manual.* Spencer, Indiana: Spencer Evening World. Miller, W.R., and Rollnick, S. (1991). *Motivational Interviewing: Preparing People to Change Addictive Behavior.* New York: Guilford Press. Selver, M.L. (1971). *The Michigan Alcohol Screening Test: The quest for a new diagnostic instrument.* American Journal of Psychiatry, 127, 1653–1658.Skinner, H.A. (1982). *The Drug Abuse Screening Test.* Addictive Behaviors, 7, 363–371.Starke, R., and Hathaway, et al. (1942). *University of Minnesota:* University Press. Tarasoff V. Regents of University of California, 17 Cal. 3d 425, 551, P.2d 334, 131 Cal. Rptr. 14. 1976.Webster, Douglas, Eaves and Hart. (1997). *Historical, Clinical, Risk Assessment*

Chapter 3

United States Bureau of Justice Statistics. (1992). *Drugs, crime, and the justice system: A national report from the Bureau of Justice Statistics.* Washington, DC: NCJ-133652.

Chapter 4

Antonowicz, D, and Ross, R. (1994). *Essential Components of Successful Rehabilitation Programs for Offenders.* International Journal of Offender Therapy and Comparative Criminology. 38 (2), 97–104.Belenko and Peugh, (1998). *Substance Abuse and American Prison Population.* New York: National Center on Addiction and Substance Abuse at Columbia University. Ormont, L. (1988). *The Group Therapy Experience: From Theory to Practice.* International Journal of Group Psychotherapy. 38 (1) 29–45.Reid, S.T. (1981). *The Correctional System: An Introduction.* New York: Holt, Rinehart, and Winston. Schiff, J. (1975). *The Cathexis Reader.* New York: Harper and Row. Wanberg and Milkman. (1998). *Criminal Conduct and Substance Abuse Treatment: Strategies for Self Improvement and Change.* Thousand Oaks, CA: Sage Publications.

Chapter 5

Beck, A.T. (1976). *Cognitive Therapy and the Emotional Disorders.* New York: International Universities Press. Berne, E. (1964). *Games People Play.* New York: Grove. Berne, E. (1975). *What do you say after you say hello.* New York: Grove. Berne, E. (1966). *Principles of Group Treatment.* New York: Grove. Blatner, A, and Blatner, A. (1997). *The Art of Play: Helping Adults Reclaim Imagination and Spontaneity.* New York: Brunner-Routledge. Deisler, F. (2000). *Journal of Forensic Group Psychotherapy.* Vol. 28, 263–269.Dryden, W, and Di Guiseppe, (1990).*A Primer on Rational Emotive Behavioral Therapy.* Chicago: Research Press. Ellis, A. (1973). *Humanistic psychotherapy.* New York: Julian Ellis, A. (1977). *Reason and emotion in psychotherapy.* Secaucus, NJ: Citadel. Glasser, W. (1965). *Reality Therapy: A new approach to psychiatry.* New York: Harper and Row. Jeffries, (1998). *The Processing.* In M. Karp, P. Holmes, and K. Bradshaw-Tauvon (Eds.) *Handbook of*

Psychodrama, 189-202. London: Routledge. Lazarus, A. (1959). *Multi-modal Behavior Therapy.* Springer series in behavior modification. Vol. 1.Moreno, Z.T. (1972). *Beyond Aristotle, Breuer and Freud:* Moreno's contribution to the concept of catharsis. Group Psychotherapy and Psychodrama, XXIV. 1-2, p.34–43.Pearson, F.S, Lipton, D.S, Cleland, C.M, and Yee, D.S. (2002). *Effects of Cognitive-behavioral Programs on Recidivism.* Crime and Delinquency, 48 (3) 476–496.Wilson, D.B, Bouffard, L.A, and McKenzie, D.L. (2005). *A Quantitative Review of Structured Group Oriented Cognitive-behavioral Programs for Offenders.* Criminal Justice and Behavior 32, 172–204.Yalom, I.D. (1975). *The Theory and Practice of Group Psychotherapy.* New York: Basic Books.

Chapter 6

Association for Specialists in Group Work, (1998). *Association for Specialists in Group Work Best Practice Guidelines.* Journal for Specialists in Group Work, 23, 237–244.Corey, G. (1998). *Groups: Process and Practices* (5th ed.). Pacific Grove, CA: Brooks-Cole. Corey, G., and Corey, M.S., and Haynes, R. (2000). *Student Workbook for evolution of a group.* Pacific Grove, CA: Brooks-Cole. Friedman, H.W. (1989). *Practical Group Therapy.* San Francisco: Jossey-Bass, Inc. Martin, D, Garske, J, and Davis, M. (2000). *Relation of The Therapeutic Alliance With Aftercare and Other Variables: A Meta-Analytic Review.* Journal of Consulting and Clinical Psychology, 68, 438–450.Parker, J., Clevenger, J., Sherman, J. (1997). *The Psychotherapist-Patient Privilege in Group Therapy.* Journal of Group Psychotherapy, Psychodrama and Sociometry. 49 (4), 157–161.Piper, W.F, Ogrodniczuk,

J.S. (2004). *Differences in Men's and Women's Responses to Short-term Psychotherapy*. Psychotherapy Research 14 (2) 231–243.Rutan and Stone, (1984). *Group Psychotherapy Today*. Contemporary Psychiatry, (3), 1, 74–75.Vannicelli, M., (2001). *Leader Dilemmas and Countertransference Considerations in Group Psychotherapy with Substance Abusers*. International Journal of Group Psychotherapy. 51 (1): 43–62Wheelan, S.A., Davidson, B., and Tilin, F. (2003). *Group Development Across Time: Reality or Illusion ?* Small Group Research, 34, 223–245.

Chapter 7

Abel, G., et al.(1985). *Sexual Offenders: Results of Assessment and Recommendations for Treatment*. Clinical Criminology: The Assessment and Treatment of Criminal Behavior. Toronto: Clarke Institute of Psychiatry, University of Toronto. Brown, S., Yalom, I. (1977). *Interactional Group Therapy with Alcoholics.* Journal of Studies on Alcohol. 38 (3), 426–456.Grossman, L.S. (1985). *Research Directions in the Evaluation and Treatment of Sex Offenders: An Analysis*, Behavioral Sciences, 50 (3), 421–440.Groth, N. (1982). *Handbook of Clinical Intervention in Child Sexual Abuse*. Lexington, MA: Lexington Books. Holtzworth-Munroe, A., and Stuart, G.L. (1994). *Typologies of Male Batterers: Three Subtypes and the Differences Among Them*. Psychological Bulletin, 116 (3), 476–497. Laws, D.R. (1999). *Relapse Prevention: The State of the Art.* Journal of Interpersonal Violence, 14 (3), 285–302.Marshall, W.L., et al. (1991). *Issues in Clinical Practice with Sexual Offenders*. Journal of Interpersonal Violence, 6 (1), 68–93.Marshall, W.L., and Pithers, W.D. (1994). *A Reconsideration of Treatment Outcome with Sex*

Offenders. Criminal Justice and Behavior, 21 (1), 10–27. Pithers, W.D. (1990). *Relapse Prevention with Sexual Aggressors: A Method for Maintaining Therapeutic Gain and Enhancing External Supervision.* In W.L. Marshall, D.R. Laws, and H.E. Barbaree (Eds.), Handbook of Sexual Assault: Issues, Theory, and Treatment of the Offender, (pg. 343–361). New York: Plenum Press. Rice, M., Harris, G.T., and Quinsey, V.L. (1990). *A Follow-up of Rapists Assessed in a Maximum Security Psychiatric Facility.* Journal of Interpersonal Violence. 5, 435–448. Zonana, H. (1997). *Cited in Are Sex Offenders Treatable,* L.S. Grossman, B. Martis, and C.G. Fichner, Psychiatric Service. 50, 349–361.

Chapter 8

Alverson H, Alverson M, Drake R.E. (2001). *Social Patterns of Substance use Among People with Dual Diagnoses.* Mental Health Services Research 3:3–14. Bradizza, C.M, Stasiewicz, P.R, and Carey, K.B. (1998). *High Risk Alcohol and Drug use Situations Among Seriously Mentally Ill Patients: A Preliminary Investigation.* Addictive Behaviors, 23, 555–560.Bradizza, C.M, and Stasiewicz, P.R. (2003). *Qualitative Analysis of High Risk Drug and Alcohol Use Situations Among Seriously Mentally Ill Substance Abusers.* Addictive Behaviors, 28, 157–169. Carich, M.S. (1997). *Relapse Prevention.* Unpublished manuscript. Davis, K.E, and O'Neill, S.J. (2005). *A Focus Group Analysis of Relapse Prevention Strategies for Persons with Substance Abuse and Mental Disorders.* Psychiatric Services 56: 1288–1291.Goodwin, F.K, Jamison, K.R. (1990). *Manic Depressive Illness.* New York: Oxford University Press. Gorski, T.T. (1990). *The Cenaps Model of Relapse Prevention: Basic Principles and Procedures.* Journal of Psychoactive Drugs, 22, 125–133.Marlatt, G.A, and Gordon, J.R. (1985). *Relapse Prevention: Maintenance Strategies in the Treatment of Addictive Behaviors.* New York: Guilford. McGovern M.P, Wrisley B.R, Drake R.E. (2005). *Relapse of substance use disorder and its prevention among persons with co-occurring disorders:* Psychiatric Services 56: 1270–1273.

Chapter 9

American Psychological Association. (1995). *Ethical Principles of Psychologists and Code of Conduct.* Washington, DC: Author. (Available online: www.apa.org/ethicscode. html.)Corey, G., Corey, M.S., and Callahan, P. (2000). *Issues and Ethics in the Helping Professions.* Pacific Grove, CA: Brooks-Cole. Deisler, F.J. (2004). *Confidentiality Issues Counseling Criminal Justice Clients.* Journal of Forensic Counseling. Lowenberg, F.M., Dolgoff, R. and Harrington, D. (2000). *Guidelines for Ethical Decision Making.* In Ethical Decisions for Social Work Practice. (pp. 43–77) Itasca, Il: F. E. Peacock, Publishers, Inc. Marshall, W.L., D. Anderson, and Y. Fernandez. (1999). *Cognitive-behavioral Treatment of Sexual Offenders:* John Wiley and Sons. Meichenbaum, D., and Turk, D. (1987). *Treatment nonadherence: A Practitioner's Guidebook.* New York: Plenum Press. Petrila, J.P., and Sadoff, R.L. (1992). *Confidentiality and the family as caregiver.* Hospital and Community Psychiatry 43, 136–139.